THIS IS HISTORY!

The Holocaust

A KEY STAGE 3 DEPTH STUDY

ANN

MOORE

CHRISTOPHER

CULPIN

Hodder Murray

A MEMBER OF THE HODDER HEADLINE GROUP

The Schools History Project

The Project was set up in 1972, with the aim of improving the study of History for students aged 13–16. This involved a reconsideration of the ways in which History contributes to the educational needs of young people. The Project devised new objectives, new criteria for planning and developing courses, and the materials to support them. New examinations, requiring new methods of assessment, also had to be developed. These have continued to be popular. The advent of GCSE in 1987 led to the expansion of Project approaches into other syllabuses.

The Schools History Project has been based at Trinity and All Saints College, Leeds, since 1978, from where it supports teachers through a biennial Bulletin, regular INSET, an annual conference and a website (www.tasc.ac.uk/shp).

Since the National Curriculum was drawn up in 1991, the Project has continued to expand its publications, bringing its ideas to courses for Key Stage 3 as well as a range of GCSE and A level specifications.

Note: The wording and sentence structure of some written sources have been adapted and simplified to make them accessible to all pupils, while faithfully preserving the sense of the original.

Words printed in SMALL CAPITALS are defined in the Glossary on page 62.

© Ann Moore and Christopher Culpin 2003

First published in 2003
by Hodder Murray, a division of Hodder Headline Ltd
338 Euston Road
London NW1 3BH

Reprinted in 2005, 2006

Layouts by Amanda Hawkes
Artwork by Oxford Illustrators, Tony Randell
Typeset in Goudy by Wearset Ltd, Boldon, Tyne and Wear
Printed and bound in Great Britain by CPI Bath

A catalogue entry for this book is available from the British Library

Pupils' Book ISBN-10: 0 7195 7709 8
ISBN-13: 978 0 7195 7709 3
Teachers' Resource Book ISBN-10: 0 7195 7710 1
ISBN-13: 978 0 7195 7710 9

◆ Contents

INTRODUCTION

Find out about the damage caused by stereotyping

◆ Stereotypes

Images like those shown on the T-shirt in Source 1 are called *stereotypes*. Stereotypes are false or do not tell the whole truth. Often we have a stereotypical view of people from another country or another culture. When we meet them we soon realise that they don't fit the stereotype.

DISCUSS

Study Source 1.

1 What assumptions has the cartoonist made about each of the nationalities? List words associated with each image.
2 Why might stereotypes like this be harmful?

Stereotypes may sometimes seem funny but they are also dangerous because some people never try to look beyond them. When this happens, the stereotype leads to PREJUDICE. Prejudice leads to hatred. Hatred leads to cruelty. The Holocaust is one example of this process in action.

SOURCE 1   A cartoonist's view, on the front of a T-shirt, of twelve nations of the European Union.

4

ACTIVITY

The right to be different!
If you chose two people from your class at random you could probably come up with at least twenty differences between them. You could also come up with twenty similarities, but it is the differences that make life interesting.

Unfortunately history has shown that it is also sometimes quite dangerous to be different. Here are some examples from the past 2500 years of individuals who have suffered because they had different beliefs, different habits or different religions from others. See if you can match each person (1–7) with the correct consequence (A–G).

1 **Galileo Galilei** – Italian scientist. In the 1630s, his study of the stars made him sure that the Christian Church was wrong to claim that the Earth was at the centre of the universe. He wrote a book showing that the Sun was at the centre of the solar system.

A He was made to drink poison for trying to make people think in a new way.

B All ETHNIC Albanians like her were forced to leave Kosovo. Thousands were murdered.

C He was imprisoned and tortured to death for refusing to convert.

D His books were banned. He was sentenced to prison unless he recanted (said that he was wrong).

E He and other Jewish leaders in Hrubieszow were rounded up and shot.

F He and all the others were arrested, found guilty of necromancy (communicating with the dead) and executed.

G She was sent to the guillotine (executed).

2 Samuel Halevi – chief tax collector and valued adviser to Pedro the Cruel, King of Castile (in Spain). Pedro was a Catholic. In 1361 he ordered all Jews, like Samuel, to become Christians ('conversos'), or else he would take away their land. Samuel refused.

3 Socrates – Greek philosopher. Around 400BC he introduced his method of thinking (Socratic philosophy). He said that you should not accept something just because it had always been done that way. Instead you should test old ideas by asking questions.

4 Thomas Baillie – Gypsy leader. In 1596, a band of travelling English Gypsies met together in Yorkshire to do SORCERY and magic, as they and their families had done for many years.

5 Olympe de Gouges – a butcher's daughter from Montauban in France. In 1791 she was angry that women were not part of the government. She published a book called *The Rights of Woman*.

6 Valboxa Paj a Ziti – a mother in Kosovo in eastern Europe. In 1999 she was one of thousands of Albanians whose families had lived in Kosovo for many years. The Serbian government wanted to make sure that Kosovo contained only Serbs.

7 Zvi Scherer – engineer. In the 1930s Zvi was one of over 3 million Jews living in Poland. He lived in Hrubieszow (pronounced 'Hrubyeshov'). In 1939 German NAZIS – who hated Jews – invaded his city.

◆ The Holocaust

In this book you will learn about the Holocaust. This is the name given to the killing by German Nazis of Jews and others during the Second World War. Jewish people also call this event the Shoah.

Adolf Hitler and his Nazi Party hated the Jews and wanted to get rid of them. But they also wanted to get rid of Gypsies, homosexuals, Jehovah's Witnesses, mentally or physically disabled people and anyone else who they thought was different. During twelve years of Nazi rule, around 6 million Jews, at least 200,000 Gypsies and countless numbers of other innocent people were killed by Nazis following Hitler's orders.

◆ The testimony of Regina Scherer: part 1

How can a textbook help you to understand these events, involving such huge numbers of people?

Every one of those killed was unique. So one way to approach the Holocaust is to look at how just one person was affected. At several points in this book, therefore, you will read the TESTIMONY of a Jewish woman called Regina Scherer. This will be in her own words.

Regina was one of four children. Her brothers and sisters all died during the Holocaust. At the end of the Second World War, Regina was in Bergen-Belsen CONCENTRATION CAMP. Among those who freed the people in the camp was a British soldier whom Regina later married. She moved to Coventry in England and had two children. Before she died in March 1996 she told her friends about some of her experiences and recorded some of them. Source 2 begins the story.

SOURCE 2 Regina Scherer in 1995

I was born on 15 July 1926 in the city of Hrubieszow in Poland. My mother Rosalin and father Zvi were relatively well off since Father was a civil engineer. Father was ten years older than Mother who was only 21 when I was born. They were very much in love. Mother always said that Father was her best friend as well as her husband. Next door to us lived Grandfather Shlomo as he was called. He was a very clever man and had been a university lecturer.

I had two sisters and one brother: Helena, Sasha, my brother, and finally Bracha, my favourite, who was born in 1934. Mother was 29 by then but she was still young enough to play with us all and give us treats of fruit or home-made ice cream.

I adored my father. He was such a good-looking man, and when I went out with him I would feel like a queen or princess.

◆ *Your big task: create and design your own web pages to build a Holocaust evidence website*

As a fairly recent historical event, there is plenty of evidence about the Holocaust.

Through most of this book you will have one main task. You will choose items of evidence to go on a website for teenagers, which is aimed at helping them to investigate the Holocaust.

The work that you do in your exercise books or folders will be recorded and designed as web pages. Eventually you could load these web pages onto your own, your class, or your school website. You could use the homepage shown here, or design a similar one.

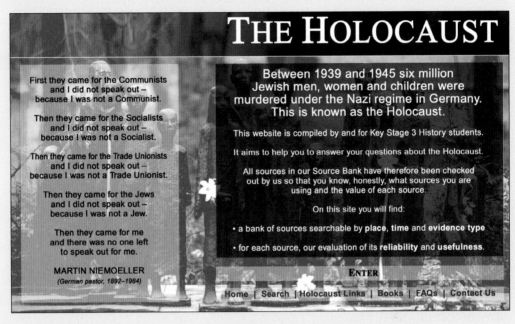

THE HOLOCAUST

First they came for the Communists and I did not speak out – because I was not a Communist.

Then they came for the Socialists and I did not speak out – because I was not a Socialist.

Then they came for the Trade Unionists and I did not speak out – because I was not a Trade Unionist.

Then they came for the Jews and I did not speak out – because I was not a Jew.

Then they came for me and there was no one left to speak out for me.

MARTIN NIEMOELLER
(German pastor, 1892–1984)

Between 1939 and 1945 six million Jewish men, women and children were murdered under the Nazi regime in Germany. This is known as the Holocaust.

This website is compiled by and for Key Stage 3 History students.

It aims to help you to answer your questions about the Holocaust.

All sources in our Source Bank have therefore been checked out by us so that you know, honestly, what sources you are using and the value of each source.

On this site you will find:

• a bank of sources searchable by **place**, **time** and **evidence type**

• for each source, our evaluation of its **reliability** and **usefulness**.

ENTER

Home | Search | Holocaust Links | Books | FAQs | Contact Us

There are already many websites about the Holocaust. What will be different about yours?

◆ **Yours will be *well organised***
Visitors must be able to search the sources on your site by:
- **place**
- **time**
- **evidence type**.

◆ **Yours will be *honest***
The Holocaust is a controversial topic. Some Holocaust websites are full of PROPAGANDA. So beware! Your website will say exactly what you are trying to do and why.

◆ **Yours will *evaluate* the evidence**
You are serious Key Stage 3 pupils. You know that you have to check the **reliability** of historical sources before you decide how **useful** they are going to be. So your website will be different because each web page will provide **evaluations** of each item of evidence you include.

To evaluate a source you have to ask: WHO made this source? WHY did they make it? WHEN did they make it? WHAT are they saying?

Sometimes you will not be able to answer all of these questions – the information is not always available – but try to answer as many as possible. You will then be able to evaluate how **reliable** and how **useful** the source is for studying that aspect of the Holocaust.

2. WHAT WAS IT LIKE TO BE JEWISH IN EUROPE IN THE 1930s?

Investigate the Jewish way of life in Europe before the Nazis took power in Germany

In the 1930s there were thriving Jewish communities all over Europe (see Source 1). They differed from country to country and place to place. There was no such thing as a 'typical' Jewish community. However, there were usually some common features.

Wherever they lived most Jews tried to keep alive their religion and customs. They studied Hebrew. They built synagogues, said their special prayers and joined together for their special meals. They took a particular interest in education and set up schools. They had their own newspapers, clubs and charities to look after the poor.

Many also took a full part as citizens in the life of the country they were living in. There were Jewish factory-owners, industrialists and railway developers. There were doctors, teachers and shopkeepers. But there were also poor Jewish workers and farmers.

In the First World War, Jews were called up into the armies of all the opposing nations: Jews fought for France, Britain, Italy and Russia on one side and for Germany, Austria-Hungary and Turkey on the other. In fighting for Germany, 12,000 Jews were killed.

Sources 2–5 show you what you might have seen, or stories you might have heard, if you had visited Jewish communities around Europe in the 1930s.

SOURCE 1 The Jewish populations of the countries of Europe in the 1930s (total: 7,870,788). Jews killed in the Holocaust came from all of the countries named.

N

0   500 km

Norway 1,728
Denmark 5,577
Netherlands 139,687
Belgium 90,000
Estonia 4,566
Latvia 93,479
USSR 1,300,000
Lithuania 153,743
Germany 554,000
Poland 3,225,000
Czechoslovakia 356,830
France 300,000
Austria 181,778
Hungary 473,000
Italy 48,000
Yugoslavia 70,000
Romania 796,000
Albania 400
Greece 77,000

SOURCE 2 Seven Jewish children in their hometown of Nowogrodek, in Russia, in 1936. Only three of the children survived the Holocaust.

SOURCE 3 John Fox was born in Tuszyn, a small town in Poland, in 1928. Here he recalls his childhood and schooldays.

Everybody was hungry for education. I think European Jews were the most knowledgeable people on earth, because they wanted to know about the world around them. Those early years of my life were good years for me. I knew everybody by their first names and they knew me. We had a good feeling towards one another. It was our domain. Life was good.

SOURCE 5 The 'New Synagogue' in Berlin, Germany, opened in 1866.

SOURCE 4 Thriving Jewish quarter in Krakow, Poland, August 1933.

ACTIVITY

Choose one photograph and work with a partner to make three lists:

a) what this photo definitely tells you
b) what you can infer from this photo (things that this photo suggests might be true – even if you are not quite sure)
c) questions you have about Jewish people in the 1930s.

◆ The testimony of Regina Scherer: part 2

Let us go back to Regina, whom you met on page 6. Regina is the person whose story we are going to follow throughout this book.

What were her experiences of growing up as a Jew in Poland?

ACTIVITY

Read Source 2 from page 6 again, then read Source 6 below. As you read more about Regina think about the following questions:
a) Was she leading a normal life?
b) How useful is her testimony for finding out about Jews across Europe in the 1930s?

SOURCE 6

We were living in a country that was traditionally hostile towards the Jews.

I remember the matter which so enraged me when I was nine or ten was the knowledge that I would not be able to go to the same grammar school as my Catholic counterparts because Polish Jews were not given the same freedom of choice as Polish Catholics. Neither Father nor Grandfather shirked [avoided] my questions. Both tried to explain how such hatred had come about. I learned that the Jews had apparently committed 'Deicide' [killed God]. This was difficult to understand since I knew that all Christians, Jews and Muslims believed that God was always present.

There were no Jewish schools in Poland so I went to school with the Polish and Ukrainian Catholics, the Russian Orthodox children and the other Jewish children. In the main, the school teachers themselves treated us fairly. One or two of them ignored the Jews in the class and always gave the best books or jobs to the Catholics. I remember our geography teacher was a bit like this. Others, however, treated us just the same. They were always the best teachers too. Perhaps they didn't need to feel as superior as the not so good teachers?

The only real trouble in school came directly after religion lessons. We were separated into three different groups, Catholic, Russian Orthodox and Jew. The Catholic children had their lesson with the local priest. After each lesson the Catholics would appear and begin to kick and spit at us. Of course we couldn't retaliate because that would have made matters even worse. You see, they were taught to hate the Jews by the priest who was also in charge of making sure that the school was run as a proper Catholic school. If we had retaliated we would have been expelled. This would have lost us our only chance of a proper education.

The first signs of real trouble in our town came at the beginning of 1938 when I was eleven years old. It began with the university students who stood in front of our shops and newsagents shouting, 'Don't buy from the Jews,' so gradually the shops were forced to shut down. Things grew steadily worse.

Website task

This is your first website task. You can look back to page 7 to remind yourself of your aims if you need to. Then:

1 Choose three sources (at least one text source and one picture) from pages 8–10 to go on your website. These should be three sources which you think will most help students to know what life was like for Jewish people in Europe in the 1930s. For each source you will need to complete a record – see opposite. This will allow your sources to be searched.

2 Write a paragraph based on Sources 1–6 describing what it was like to be Jewish in Europe in the 1930s.

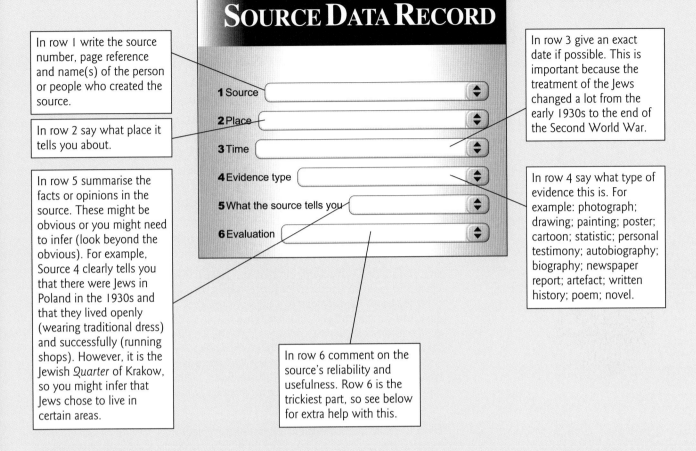

In row I write the source number, page reference and name(s) of the person or people who created the source.

In row 2 say what place it tells you about.

In row 5 summarise the facts or opinions in the source. These might be obvious or you might need to infer (look beyond the obvious). For example, Source 4 clearly tells you that there were Jews in Poland in the 1930s and that they lived openly (wearing traditional dress) and successfully (running shops). However, it is the Jewish *Quarter* of Krakow, so you might infer that Jews chose to live in certain areas.

In row 3 give an exact date if possible. This is important because the treatment of the Jews changed a lot from the early 1930s to the end of the Second World War.

In row 4 say what type of evidence this is. For example: photograph; drawing; painting; poster; cartoon; statistic; personal testimony; autobiography; biography; newspaper report; artefact; written history; poem; novel.

In row 6 comment on the source's reliability and usefulness. Row 6 is the trickiest part, so see below for extra help with this.

How to fill out row 6

Step A: think about the pluses and minuses of this type of source

For example:

◆ A photograph usually shows you something that actually happened, but it's not true to say that 'the camera never lies' because photos can be posed (see Source 2), or altered.
◆ A photo shows only one place at one moment so it needs to be cross-referenced with other photos or accounts to see if it is typical.

No source is reliable or unreliable simply because of the type of source it is. So you need to be more specific.

Step B: think about whether this *particular* source helps you to answer a *particular* question

You are interested in whether Jews in the 1930s were living normal lives. You choose a source that appears to be useful for this topic, but is it reliable? Do you trust this source to tell you honestly about the life of Jews in the 1930s? Does anything about this source make you suspicious? Do you think it was made to put forward a particular message? Or can you take it at face value? For example, for Source 4 you might say:
Photographs can be posed but this one looks natural, which makes us think it gives reliable evidence that Jews in 1930s Poland were not being PERSECUTED.

Remember
◆ Look at, or read, a source very carefully.
◆ Usefulness and reliability go together. Whether something is useful depends on whether it is reliable. Whether something is reliable depends on what you are using it for. The words 'what … for' are very important.
◆ The same source can be reliable for one use (e.g. finding out whether there were Jews there) but unreliable for another use (e.g. finding out *how many* Jews were there).

HOW DID ANTI-SEMITISM CHANGE THROUGH HISTORY?

Uncover the roots of anti-Semitism

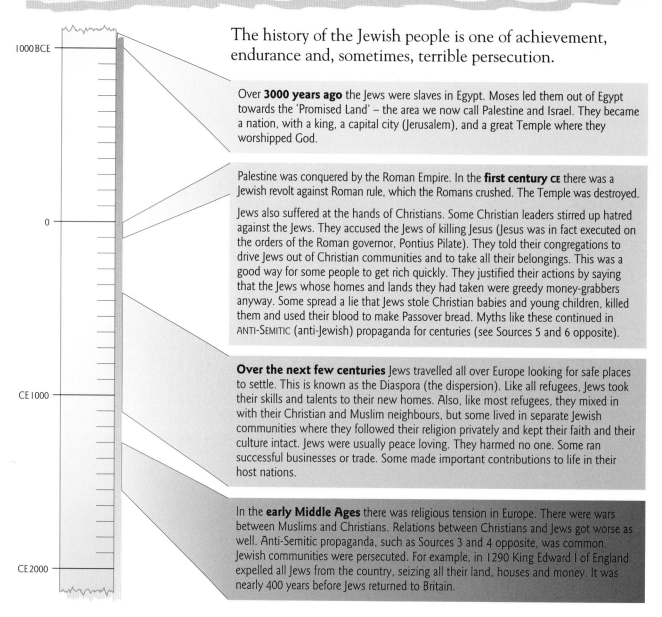

The history of the Jewish people is one of achievement, endurance and, sometimes, terrible persecution.

1000 BCE

Over **3000 years ago** the Jews were slaves in Egypt. Moses led them out of Egypt towards the 'Promised Land' – the area we now call Palestine and Israel. They became a nation, with a king, a capital city (Jerusalem), and a great Temple where they worshipped God.

0

Palestine was conquered by the Roman Empire. In the **first century CE** there was a Jewish revolt against Roman rule, which the Romans crushed. The Temple was destroyed.

Jews also suffered at the hands of Christians. Some Christian leaders stirred up hatred against the Jews. They accused the Jews of killing Jesus (Jesus was in fact executed on the orders of the Roman governor, Pontius Pilate). They told their congregations to drive Jews out of Christian communities and to take all their belongings. This was a good way for some people to get rich quickly. They justified their actions by saying that the Jews whose homes and lands they had taken were greedy money-grabbers anyway. Some spread a lie that Jews stole Christian babies and young children, killed them and used their blood to make Passover bread. Myths like these continued in ANTI-SEMITIC (anti-Jewish) propaganda for centuries (see Sources 5 and 6 opposite).

CE 1000

Over the next few centuries Jews travelled all over Europe looking for safe places to settle. This is known as the Diaspora (the dispersion). Like all refugees, Jews took their skills and talents to their new homes. Also, like most refugees, they mixed in with their Christian and Muslim neighbours, but some lived in separate Jewish communities where they followed their religion privately and kept their faith and their culture intact. Jews were usually peace loving. They harmed no one. Some ran successful businesses or trade. Some made important contributions to life in their host nations.

CE 2000

In the **early Middle Ages** there was religious tension in Europe. There were wars between Muslims and Christians. Relations between Christians and Jews got worse as well. Anti-Semitic propaganda, such as Sources 3 and 4 opposite, was common. Jewish communities were persecuted. For example, in 1290 King Edward I of England expelled all Jews from the country, seizing all their land, houses and money. It was nearly 400 years before Jews returned to Britain.

ACTIVITY

How were Jews described in anti-Semitic propaganda?

Sources 1–6 on page 13 are all anti-Semitic propaganda. They are all totally unreliable for telling you about the Jews but are still quite useful for telling you about anti-Semitism over the centuries.

Copy and complete a table like this to analyse the sources.

Source	Place	Time	Evidence type	What accusation the source makes against Jews

SOURCE 1 Melito, Bishop of Sardis (Asia Minor), second century CE.

You [all the Jews] killed the Lord in the middle of Jerusalem. Hear all generations of the peoples and see ... He who created the universe was himself nailed to the wood. The Lord was killed. God was murdered. The King of Israel was murdered by Jewish hands. Oh, this unheard of murder. Oh, this unheard of injustice.

▲ **SOURCE 2** Copy of a drawing by an Italian monk in 1023 of Jews holding their hands over their ears because they did not want to listen to the Christian gospel.

SOURCE 3 ▶ A statue from Strasbourg Cathedral, France, 1230–40. The figure, representing the Jewish faith, is shown holding a book of the Tables of the Law (the basis of JUDAISM) but is also blindfolded (unable to 'see' Christianity) and is holding a broken lance (so is powerless).

SOURCE 4 From the thirteenth-century Syrian Arab writer Abd al Rahim al Jawbari.

They [the Jews] are the most evil natured and most deeply rooted in falseness and accursedness. They are the most evil intentioned of mankind in their deeds even though they are the most showy in humility and being humble. When they manage to be alone with a man they bring him to destruction. They introduce by trickery a stupefying drug to the food and then they kill him.

▲ **SOURCE 5** A German woodcut, 1493, illustrating the story of the murder of the young German boy Simon of Trent, supposedly by Jews wanting his blood to make Passover bread. Simon was later made a saint.

▲ **SOURCE 6** 'The greedy, money-grabbing Jew' (a moneylender), drawn in Manchester in 1773.

13

◆ Anti-Semitism after 1850

Most of the anti-Semitic propaganda you have looked at so far on page 13 was based on religion. In the mid-nineteenth century new ideas were put forward based on race. These ideas were popular among some Germans, who were told that they belonged to the 'superior' ARYAN race, while Jews were Semitic, an 'inferior' race. The German composer Richard Wagner included these ideas in some of his operas.

Magazines like *Ostara* (see Source 7) put forward such views. Its readers included the young Adolf Hitler.

Other writers thought up a 'race science', which claimed to identify physical characteristics of 'superior' and 'inferior' races (see Source 8).

SOURCE 8 A diagram from a German 'race science' book, showing racially superior and inferior bottoms. (B is supposedly superior.)

SOURCE 7 Title page of the German magazine *Ostara*, around 1900. The main text reads: 'Germans! Who must lead, who must be duke?' Underneath the name *Ostara* it calls itself a 'library for blonds'.

SOURCE 9

A postcard from Germany before the First World War. It advertises a 'Jew-free hotel' in Frankfurt and shows a Jew, who wished to stay there, being kicked out of the building.

Website task

1 Add Sources 7–9 to your table from page 12.

2 a) Choose four sources from Sources 1–9 for your website. (At least one source must be from before 1850 and at least one from after 1850.) They should help readers to answer the question: How did anti-Semitism change through history?

b) For each of your chosen sources complete a source data record. The details in your table will help you.

SOURCE DATA RECORD

1 Source

2 Place

3 Time

4 Evidence type

5 What the source tells you

6 Evaluation

If you need advice on filling this out, look back to page 11.

◆ Hitler's anti-Semitism

Adolf Hitler was born in 1889. As a young man he lived in Vienna, where anti-Semitic ideas were very common. He read magazines like *Ostara* (see Source 7 on page 14).

Hitler fought in the First World War. He was an ordinary frontline soldier. He was gassed. When the war ended he was bitterly disillusioned. Like many Germans he could not believe that Germany had lost the war. He blamed the weak government for giving in and for signing the Treaty of Versailles. This made Germany pay in many ways for starting the war.

He decided to get involved in politics. He joined the tiny German Workers' Party in 1919. It had only six members. He soon became its leader and changed its name to the National Socialist German Workers' Party, or Nazis for short.

Hitler became a skilled public speaker in the Munich beer-halls where the party held its meetings.

The 25 Points

In 1920 the Nazis drew up policies for the time when they might have power. The main policies were known as the 25 Points.

SOURCE 10 Two of the Nazis' 25 Points, 1920.

4 Only members of the nation can be citizens of the state. Only a person of German blood can be a member of the nation. No Jew, therefore, can be a member of the nation.
5 Anyone who is not a citizen of the state may live in Germany only as a guest.

SOURCE 11 C. Zuckmayer, an early Nazi supporter, describing Nazi rallies in the early 1920s. He was writing his memoirs in 1938 after Hitler had become the leader of Germany.

Hitler knew how to whip up those crowds jammed closely in a dense cloud of cigarette smoke – not by argument, but by his manner: the roaring and screeching and especially the power of repetition delivered in a certain infectious rhythm ... He would draw up a list of real or imaginary evils and abuses and scream, in higher and higher crescendo: 'And whose fault is it? It's all ... the fault ... of the Jews!'

The beer-mugs would swiftly take up the beat, crashing down on the wooden tables, and hundreds of voices, shrill and female or male beer-bellied, repeated the idiotic line.

SOURCE 12 Photographs of Hitler practising public speaking, in 1927. The photos helped him see which of his gestures looked most dramatic.

DISCUSS A

1 How reliable is Source 11 as evidence of Hitler's ability as a speaker?
2 How useful is this source for finding out about Hitler's anti-Semitism?
3 How useful is this source for finding out about anti-Semitism in Germany?

◆ *Mein Kampf*

In 1925 Hitler published a book about his life and ideas called *Mein Kampf* (*My Struggle*). He repeated many of the anti-Jewish ideas that were common at the time. He also added his own attacks on the Jews. He blamed Jews for almost anything that he found wrong in Germany.

SOURCE 13   Hitler's anti-Semitic views in *Mein Kampf*, 1925, alongside the front cover of the first edition.

A 'The unclean Jew'

The cleanliness of this people, moral and otherwise, I must say is a point in itself. I often grew sick to my stomach from the smell of these caftan [long-sleeved robe] wearers. In addition to their physical uncleanliness, you discovered the moral stains of this 'chosen people'.

... Was there any form of filth or profligacy [excess], particularly in cultural life, without at least one Jew involved in it?

... If you cut even cautiously into such an abscess, you found [the Jew] like a maggot in a rotting body, often dazzled by the sudden light.

B 'The Jews and Negroes who defile the white race'

With satanic joy in his face, the black haired Jewish youth lurks in wait for the unsuspecting girl whom he defiles with his blood, thus stealing her from her people. With every means he tries to destroy the racial foundation of the people he has set out to control. It was and is the Jews who bring the Negroes into the Rhineland, always with the same secret thought and clear aim of ruining the hated white race by the necessarily resulting bastardisation.

C 'The end of the Jews'

The aim is not only the freedom of the peoples oppressed by the Jew, but also the end of this parasite upon the nations. After the death of his victim, the vampire sooner or later dies too.

D I S C U S S B

1 Are Hitler's anti-Semitic views in Source 13 more extreme than the views expressed in Sources 1–6 on p.13?

2 Hitler's book, *Mein Kampf*, is still in print. Its publishers, Pimlico Books, say:
'It is essential reading for all students of twentieth-century history and its existence reminds us that we must remain vigilant if its evil creed is to be contained.'
However, one adviser on this textbook asked us not to include the quotes in Source 13, saying:
'They might incite racial hatred.'
With whom do you agree, our adviser or Pimlico Books? Were we wrong or right to include these quotes?

3 Would you put any of *Mein Kampf* on your website? If so, you know what to do by now – fill out a source data record (see page 11).

◆ *Did Hitler's anti-Semitism help him to power?*

In 1923 Hitler tried to take over Germany by force. This was called the Munich PUTSCH. He failed. Hardly anyone supported the Nazis. He was arrested, tried and put in prison.

When he came out of prison, he decided to change his methods. Instead of taking over by violence, the Nazis would try to get elected. To start with, few Germans took his kind of views seriously. In the 1928 elections less than three per cent of Germans voted Nazi.

Yet, just five years later, the situation had changed completely. The Nazis were the biggest party and Hitler, the EXTREMIST, was ruler of one of the most advanced (and most democratic) countries in the world.

This was an extraordinary turnaround. How do we explain it? Some historians have spent their lives trying to do so!

Here is a summary of some historians' views.

The Treaty of Versailles
At the end of the First World War, Germany was forced to sign the Treaty of Versailles. Most Germans hated it. It took away German land, it cut back the armed forces they were so proud of and it forced them to pay massive REPARATIONS to France and Britain. Hitler promised to get rid of this Treaty, to retake German land, to re-arm Germany and to make Germany great again. Many Germans believed him.

Fear of Communism
Communists were strong in Germany. They had nearly taken over in 1918 and many Germans feared they would try to do so again. The Germans could see what that meant just by looking at Russia. The Communist government there had taken over industry and farms. The Nazis were violently anti-Communist. Hitler spoke against the Communists almost as much as he did against the Jews. He sent his supporters to break up Communist meetings and to beat up Communist supporters. He said that only the Nazis could protect Germany from the Communist threat. Many believed him.

The Great Depression
In 1929 a world-wide DEPRESSION began. Germany was badly affected. Banks went broke. Factories shut down. Millions were thrown out of work. The German government seemed unable to tackle the problem. However, Hitler promised that the Nazis would provide jobs for all Germans. Many Germans believed him.

Why did the Nazis succeed?

Hitler
Hitler himself was the Nazis' trump card. He seemed to be a strong leader in the old German tradition. Many Germans felt that a strong leader like Hitler was just what Germany needed. They believed in him.

Effective campaigning
Nazi election tactics were ahead of their time. Hitler flew all over Germany, addressing up to five mass rallies per day (this was before the days of television). The Nazis used clever propaganda. At the local level they ran soup kitchens and youth events. They matched their message to what their audiences wanted to hear. When they were talking to people who hated Jews, they promised to root out the Jews from Germany; when they were talking to people who were not worried about the Jews, they would drop that message. They discovered that it did not matter very much what they promised as long as people trusted them. If all else failed, Hitler used vague promises such as he would 'make Germany great again'. Many Germans believed him.

SOURCE 14 Nazi election poster, 1932. The farmer is saying: 'We are mucking out.' In his shovel are Communists and Jewish businessmen.

SOURCE 15 Nazi election poster, 1932. It says: 'We want work and bread! Vote for Hitler!'

ACTIVITY

1 Here are five promises Hitler was making before he came to power:

◆ To scrap the Treaty of Versailles
◆ To rebuild German armed forces
◆ To make Germany great again
◆ To provide jobs for all Germans
◆ To get rid of Jews and Communists (who, he said, were dragging Germany down).

Write a sentence for each one, explaining why it would appeal to the German people. Use the diagram on page 18 to help you.

2 Sources 14 and 15 are examples of Nazi election propaganda. On your own copy of these sources, explain their messages, using the information on pages 14–18 to help you.

3 Write a sentence explaining whether you think Hitler's anti-Semitism was
a) the *main* factor
b) *one* of the factors
c) *not* a factor
in helping Hitler to gain power.

DISCUSS

Hitler was violently anti-Semitic. Does that mean that all of the Germans who voted for the Nazis in 1933 were anti-Semitic?

4 HOW DID HITLER MAKE GERMAN JEWS INTO NON-CITIZENS?

Analyse Nazi laws to understand their impact on German Jews

◆ Hitler's first actions

On 30 January 1933 Adolf Hitler was made Chancellor (or Prime Minister) of Germany.

Many Germans did not really expect him to carry out the promises he had made. But they were in for a shock. Within months he had:

◆ removed all opposition and made himself DICTATOR of Germany – the FÜHRER
◆ begun to re-arm the country and plan for war
◆ begun to attack the Jews of Germany, both by laws taking away their rights as citizens and by violence in the streets.

Within days of becoming Chancellor, he closed down the offices and printing presses of all organisations that could oppose him. Within a month, he made it lawful to imprison people without trial. A few weeks later, he set up the first concentration camp at Dachau near Munich. Anyone who criticised Hitler could be sent to the camp.

Nazi Stormtroopers or 'brown shirts' had an important part to play in Hitler's new Germany. Their job was to frighten, threaten or beat up people who opposed Hitler or were, in his opinion, enemies of the Nazis. This included Communists, trade unionists and political opponents. It also included Jews.

The Nazi government supported and encouraged street violence against the Jews. On 1 April 1933 the Nazis organised a nationwide BOYCOTT of Jewish businesses, claiming that it was an act of revenge against critics of the Nazi regime. Stormtroopers barred the entrances to shops and the Star of David was daubed on shop windows.

Website task

1 How useful are Sources 1–4 on page 21 as evidence of:

a) Nazi anti-Semitism

b) Hitler's anti-Semitism

c) anti-Semitism among the German people?

Copy the table shown below and tick the relevant boxes.

Useful for investigating?		1	2	3	4
Nazi anti-Semitism	Yes				
	No				
Hitler's anti-Semitism	Yes				
	No				
Anti-Semitism among the German people	Yes				
	No				

2 Choose two sources from Sources 1–4 and add them to your website, filling out a source data record sheet for each one.

SOURCE DATA RECORD

1 Source

2 Place

3 Time

4 Evidence type

5 What the source tells you

6 Evaluation

SOURCE 1 A Jewish boy is forced to cut his father's beard whilst German soldiers watch, Germany, 1933.

SOURCE 2 Nazis burn books written by Jews and opponents of Nazism, 10 May 1933.

SOURCE 3 This banner in a small German village says, 'Jews are not welcome here'.

DISCUSS

What do you think Jews could have done about the events shown in Sources 1–4? Think of as many possible responses as you can. Then think about the possible consequences of each action. Your teacher can give you a sheet to help you.

SOURCE 4 In April 1935 in Leipzig, Germany, Jewish businessmen are forced to carry signs saying, 'Don't buy from Jews, shop in German businesses.'

◆ *Taking away the rights of Jews*

Over the next ten years, Hitler introduced many laws which gradually took away from the Jews of Germany their rights as German citizens. On pages 23–25 are just a few of them. There were many, many more than this.

Website task

1 Understand these laws

Look carefully at each law on pages 23–25. Find up to three laws that fit in each of the following categories:

a) Deprived Jews of a normal childhood

b) Made it impossible for Jews to earn a decent living

c) Were seen at the time as only minor nuisances that people could 'put up with'

d) Were probably serious blocks on people's lives.

2 Choose examples for the website

This section of your website is extremely important. These laws give you 'hard evidence' about Adolf Hitler's anti-Semitism. Choose one item from each category a), b), c) and d), in question 1, and add them to your website. Fill out a source data record sheet for each one.

SOURCE DATA RECORD

1 Source

2 Place

3 Time

4 Evidence type

5 What the source tells you

6 Evaluation

3 Now think about the big picture

One of the Nazis' purposes in passing these laws was to make other Germans think that Jews were not normal citizens.

a) At which point did Jews cease to be citizens of Germany? Explain your answer.

b) How did the laws make other Germans think that Jews were not normal citizens?

Support your answer with evidence from question 1. Save your answer. It will be useful for your website.

Hitler's restrictions against the Jews 1933–35

1933

March
- Jewish lawyers were forbidden to work as lawyers in Berlin
- Jewish judges were suspended from office

April
- Jewish teachers were banned from teaching in state schools
- Aryan and non-Aryan children were forbidden to play with each other
- Jewish civil servants were dismissed from public office
- Jews were excluded from sports and gymnastic clubs

1935

March
- Jewish writers were not allowed to carry out any form of literary work in Germany
- Jewish musicians were not allowed to work in state orchestras

April
- Jews were only allowed to sit on benches marked 'For Jews'
- Jewish art and antique dealers were not allowed to carry out their trade

September
The Nuremberg Laws:
- All Jews had their German citizenship removed
- Marriage ceremonies, and extramarital sex, between Germans and Jews were punishable by imprisonment
- Marriages that had already taken place were declared invalid

SOURCE 5 Stormtroopers put a couple on show in Germany, 1933. The non-Jewish woman's sign reads, 'I am the greatest swine and sleep only with Jews'. The man's sign reads, 'As a Jew boy I only take German girls up to my room'.

DISCUSS

1 What have the couple in Source 5 done wrong under the Nuremberg Laws?
2 How do you think this couple would feel: angry, afraid, humiliated, despairing or something else?

Marriage and children

On 15 September 1935, the Nuremberg Laws became law. This meant that all German Jews had their rights as citizens taken away from them. They were also banned from marrying, or having sex with, non-Jews. Non-Jewish people who were already married to Jews were forced to get divorced. This genealogical table, shown below, was drawn up to show who was affected and who wasn't.

Source 6 illustrates just how far the Nazis were prepared to take their racial ideas.

Sterilisation campaign

It wasn't just Jews whom the Nazis were worried about. A law was passed on 14 July 1933 called 'The Law for the Prevention of Offspring with Hereditary Diseases'. Between 1935 and 1939, doctors, nurses, teachers and social workers teamed up to forcibly STERILISE children and young people who were disabled in some form or other. This sterilisation programme was extended to include over 500 black teenagers and around 30,000 young Gypsies.

SOURCE 6 A genealogical table produced by the Nazis.

The diagrams below show *Who is German-blooded?* and *Who is Jewish?*. On the right are some examples of how people are to be classified according to who their grandparents were.

It sets out 'rules' for classifying people according to their race.

At the top left it says: *The law distinguishes between:* and then shows the four pairs of people.

The pair in white are *German-blooded: belong to the German blood and people and can become citizens.*

The pair shaded black are *Jews: belong to the Jewish people and are not able to become citizens.*

The next pair, in dark shading, are *Mixed race 2ⁿᵈ degree: belong solely to the German people and can become citizens.*

The last pair, lightly-shaded, on the right, are *Mixed race 1ˢᵗ degree: belong solely to the German people and can become citizens.*

The first one has three Jewish grandparents, so *Also belongs to the Jewish race.*

The next is entitled *Who is mixed race 2ⁿᵈ degree?* (three German grandparents).

The third is *Who is mixed race 1ˢᵗ degree?* (two German grandparents and two Jewish grandparents).

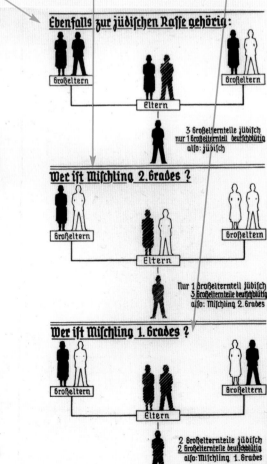

24

Hitler's restrictions against the Jews 1936–39

1936

January
- Jews had to hand over electrical and optical equipment, bicycles, typewriters and records

April
- Jewish vets were banned from working as such

August
- Anti-Jewish posters were temporarily removed during the Olympic Games which took place in Berlin

October
- Even if Jews converted to Christianity and were baptised, they were still to be classed as members of the Jewish race

1938

January
- Jews were forbidden to become members of the German Red Cross

March
- Only Aryan Germans could hold ALLOTMENTS

April
- Jews had to declare their finances so that their ASSETS could be seized by the government

July
- Non-Jews were forbidden to leave anything in their wills to Jews
- Jewish doctors were no longer allowed to work as doctors
- Jewish street names were changed

August
- Male Jews were forced to add the name 'Israel', and female Jews the name 'Sara', to their first names

October
- Jewish passports had to be stamped with a letter 'J'
- Passports of those Jews whose emigration did not suit the Nazis were seized

November
- Jews were no longer allowed to run independent businesses as craftspeople
- Jews were banned from running a retail or wholesale business
- Jews were banned from visiting cinemas, theatres, operas and concerts
- Jews were no longer allowed to buy newspapers and magazines
- Jewish children were no longer allowed to attend state schools

December
- Jews were not allowed to use open-air and indoor swimming pools
- Jews had to hand in their driving licences and vehicle permits to the police
- Jewish women were no longer able to work as midwives
- Jewish publishing houses and bookshops were closed down

1939

January
- Emigrants were not allowed to take jewellery and valuables with them
- Jewish dentists, chemists and nurses were forbidden to work as such

February
- Jews had to hand in jewellery, gold, silver, platinum and pearls to the police

March
- Jews had to collect up the ruins of their synagogues, which had been attacked by the mobs, and were forbidden to rebuild them

April
- Jews could be evicted from their homes without a reason given and without notice being served

September
- Jews were not allowed to leave their homes after 8p.m. in the winter or 9p.m. in the summer
- Jews had to hand over their radio sets

◆ *Kristallnacht*

On 6 November 1938 a young German Jewish student, Hirsch Grynspan, who was studying in Paris, received news that his parents had been beaten up by Hitler's Stormtroopers. He went to the German Embassy and shot a high-ranking official, Ernst vom Rath. Three days later vom Rath died. This unleashed an attack on Jewish property and people right across Germany.

   Over two nights, 9 and 10 November 1938, Jewish synagogues and shops were burned and looted. Altogether, 117 synagogues were destroyed, 7500 shops were looted and 91 Jews were killed. This became known as *Kristallnacht*, the 'night of the broken glass'.

SOURCE 7   Message from ss Gruppenführer Reinhard Heydrich to all State Police on 10 November 1938, after the shooting of vom Rath.

Following the attempt on the life of the Secretary of the Legation [embassy] vom Rath in Paris, demonstrations against the Jews are expected in all parts of the Reich [Germany] in the course of the coming night. The instructions below are to be applied in dealing with these events:

a) Only such measures are to be taken as do not endanger German lives or property (i.e. synagogues are to be burned down only where there is no danger of fire in neighbouring buildings).
b) Places of business and apartments belonging to Jews may be destroyed but not looted. The police are instructed to supervise the observance [obeying] of this order and to arrest looters.
c) In commercial streets particular care is to be taken that non-Jewish businesses are completely protected against damage.
d) Foreign citizens – even if they are Jews – are not to be molested [attacked].

On the assumption that the guidelines are observed, the demonstrations are not to be prevented by the police.

ACTIVITY

Your teacher will give you a copy of Source 7.

1 Underline, using one colour, all the evidence in Source 7 that Germans were to be protected on the night of *Kristallnacht*.
2 In a different colour underline all the evidence that Jews were not to receive the same protection as the Germans.

SOURCE 8 10 November 1938: the Ober Ramstadt synagogue, in Germany, in flames. The firemen prevented the fire from spreading to the home next door but did not try to save the synagogue. (The young photographer came from a family who opposed the Nazis. That day, police confiscated his film from his home. It was found in the city hall after 1945.)

SOURCE 9 10 November 1938: Germans passing the broken window of a Jewish shop in Berlin. Afterwards, all Jewish shopkeepers were forced to pay for the damage and the cleaning up that was necessary.

DISCUSS

1 What evidence in Source 7 proves that the leaders of the SS and the police were actively anti-Semitic?

2 What evidence is there in Source 7 that Heydrich does not regard German Jews as full citizens of Germany?

3 Which law from pages 23–25 allowed him to behave like this without fear of punishment?

4 How do Sources 8 and 9 support the view that Hitler's treatment of the Jews was becoming more extreme towards the end of the 1930s?

DID HITLER SUCCEED IN MAKING THE GERMANS HATE THE JEWS?

Look at the work of Goebbels – did he brainwash the Germans?

Hitler believed in 'Racial Purity'. He said that:

◆ The Germans were 'Aryans' – a superior race of people. The ideal Aryan was blue-eyed, blond-haired (although you may have noticed that Hitler himself was neither of these) and physically fit.
◆ Other races – Jews, Slavs, Gypsies and black people – were inferior and had to be rooted out of German society.
◆ To keep the racial stock pure, Aryans should not be allowed to marry or have children with members of other races.

The Nazis produced propaganda showing these ideal Germans. Sources 1–4 are examples.

This propaganda showed not only the racial ideal but also other aspects of the Nazi ideal. For example, the role of women: the Nazis believed that men should be fighters and workers; women should have babies and look after their families.

SOURCE 1 Recruitment poster for the Hitler Youth. The text reads 'Join us! Be a part of the Hitler Youth'.

HER ZU UNS!

Hinein in die Hitler-Jugend

28

SOURCE 2 Advertisement, 'Mother and Child', from a women's magazine. It reads 'Support the Mother and Child Benefit'.

SOURCE 4 The ideal German family. A Nazi community poster of 1937. It reads 'Fellow members of your community will give you advice and help, so go to your local community group'.

SOURCE 3 Recruitment poster persuading German girls to join the Hitler Youth. It says 'Build youth hostels and homes'.

◆ How did the Nazis try to impose their ideas on children?

The Nazis made a special effort to win over the hearts and minds of children, so that they would grow up to be true Nazis. The main method for INDOCTRINATING children was through the schools. The curriculum was changed to promote Nazi ideas. School teachers had to identify and publicly humiliate members of so-called 'inferior races'. If children were found to be non-Aryan, they were humiliated and driven out of the school.

SOURCE 5 The Nazi Minister for Education explained to the German people what their new education system was all about:

The chief purpose of the school is to train human beings to realise that the state is more than the individual, that individuals must be willing and ready to sacrifice themselves for Nation and Führer . . .
If students have learned to submit to authority, if they have developed a willingness to fit in to that particular place chosen for them by the Party, then their education has been successful . . .
Every girl must learn the duties of a mother before she is 16, so that she can have children. Why should girls bother with higher mathematics or art or drama or literature? They could have babies without that sort of knowledge.

SOURCE 6 Peter Beck, a former member of Hitler Youth, remembers:

It was a normal curriculum except that biology, history and geography were clearly affected by Nazi ideology. Jews were depicted [shown] in biology books as an inferior race who exploited [used] others. In biology we also learned about racial purity and race hygiene. In geography we were told how Germany had suffered and how Germany had lost its COLONIES while England, for example, was amassing its empire.
We were carefully kept from having a broad picture of history. We were not aware of what Germany had done before. Our history lessons started with the First World War and the depressing period after Germany had been beaten down as a result of the Treaty of Versailles, disarmed and saddled with reparations. We learned how Hitler came along to lift Germany out of this muck and bring it back to greatness.

SOURCE 7 A maths problem from an arithmetic book used in Nazi Germany.

The Jews are aliens in Germany. In 1933 there were 66,060,000 inhabitants of the German Reich [empire] of whom 499,682 were Jews. What is the percentage of aliens?

Front cover: The Poisonous Mushroom

Page 8: The experience of Hans and Elsa with a strange man: 'Here, children, I have some sweets for you, but you both have to come with me.'

SOURCE 8   Pages from a children's story book, published in 1938, used in reading or literacy lessons in schools in Nazi Germany. The images of the 'poisonous mushroom' and the 'strange man' are used to represent Jews.

ACTIVITY

Read Sources 5–9 then copy and complete this table.

Subject	How the Nazis used it to indoctrinate pupils

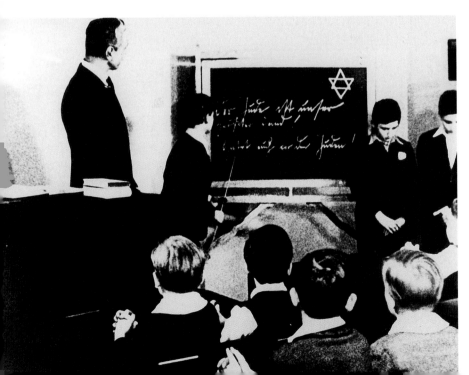

SOURCE 9   Two Jewish boys facing their class at a school in Nazi-occupied Austria, 1938. The blackboard shows the Star of David and the text reads 'The Jew is our greatest enemy. Beware of the Jew!'

Website task

Choose two sources from Sources 5–9 for your website which will help pupils trying to understand how the Nazis used school to indoctrinate young people. Complete a source data record for each source (see page 11).

◆ How did Goebbels use propaganda to indoctrinate the German people?

Hitler appointed one of his close allies, Joseph Goebbels, to be Propaganda Minister.

SOURCE 10 *Will and Way* written by Joseph Goebbels in 1931.

No other political movement has understood the art of propaganda as well as the Nazis. From its beginnings it has put heart and soul into propaganda. What distinguishes it from all other political parties is the ability to see into the soul of the people and to speak the language of the man in the street. It uses all the means of modern technology. Leaflets, handbills, posters, mass demonstrations, the press, stage, film and radio. These are all tools of our propaganda.

The essence of propaganda is not in variety, rather the forcefulness and persistence with which one selects ideas from the large pool and hammers them into the masses using the most varied methods.

SOURCE 11 A propaganda photograph of a Nazi rally at their specially built Nuremberg stadium, 1941.

ACTIVITY

On pages 32–33 are four different images created by Joseph Goebbels' Ministry of Propaganda. You are going to think about the messages about the Jews and about Hitler that Goebbels was trying to 'hammer into the masses'. Working in groups, choose one image as you did on page 28. Place a copy of it in the middle of a large piece of paper.

1 Using one colour, add labels around the image to explain the *message* of this poster – *what* impression does it give you of the Jews or of Hitler?
2 Using a second colour, add labels to explain the *method* – *how* has the artist created this impression?
3 Now choose another image and do the same again.
4 Finally, add your labelled pictures to the class display.

SOURCE 12 A poster for a film commissioned by Goebbels called *The Eternal Jew*, 1940.

SOURCE 13 A propaganda postcard showing Hitler with children.

SOURCE 14

A propaganda poster by Goebbels entitled 'Long live Germany', from the 1930s.

◆ Did the German people really hate the Jews?

The Activities on pages 28–33 analysed the Nazis' propaganda methods. You probably didn't find these too difficult. Compared to modern advertising techniques, those that Goebbels used were fairly simple. But he was the first modern propagandist. And he had almost total control of what the German people read, saw and heard. By the time the main attack on the Jews began in 1941, the German people had been fed Nazi propaganda for eight years. The young soldiers who formed the Nazi armies invading other countries in Europe had known little else since they were children. Had the Nazis brainwashed them in that time? Did the German people really hate the Jews?

The honest answer is no-one knows. It's hard to judge for sure what even one person is really thinking, let alone a nation of 66 million people! So it is not surprising that historians have been arguing about this for years. See what you think.

ACTIVITY

Sources 15–20 show the behaviour of some German people. Study the sources and then decide which of these statements is best supported by the evidence:

◆ All Germans hated Jews.
◆ Some Germans hated Jews.
◆ Nazi supporters hated Jews.

SOURCE 15 Extract from *The Path to Genocide*, by Christopher R. Browning, 1992.

Most of the [210] soldiers in Battalion 101 came from Hamburg, Germany. The average age was thirty-nine ... Very few were Nazis and none was openly anti-Semitic. Major Wilhelm Trapp ... headed the battalion.

The unit's first killing mission took place on July 13, 1942 ... the men arrived at the village of Jozefowl and assembled in a half-circle around Major Trapp, who proceeded to give a short speech. With choking voice and tears in his eyes ... he informed his men that they had received orders to perform a very unpleasant task. These orders were not to his liking, but they came from above. Trapp then explained to the men that the Jews in Jozefowl would have to be rounded up, whereupon the young males were to be selected out for labour and the others shot.

Trapp then made an extraordinary offer to his battalion: if any of the older men among them did not feel up to the task that lay before him, he could step out. Trapp paused, and after some moments, one man stepped forward. Then ten or twelve other men stepped forward as well.

SOURCE 16 A German policeman who refused to take part in killing Jews at Hrubieszow, the Polish city where Regina Scherer lived, said:

I refused because I had no desire to shoot defenceless people. I had no wish to become a murderer. I said this to my commanding officer and he did not press me further to carry out this order.

SOURCE 19 Kurt Mobius was a German police battalion member who was involved in the killing of Jews. He explained afterwards:

It never entered my head that these orders could be wrong. Although I am aware that it is the duty of the police to protect the innocent I was however at that time convinced that the Jewish people were not innocent but guilty. I believed all the propaganda that Jews were criminals and sub-human and that they were the cause of Germany's decline after the First World War . . . I followed these orders because they came from the highest leaders of the state and not because I was in any way afraid.

SOURCE 17 Max Schmeling became the first European heavyweight boxing champion of the world in 1930. He was praised by the Nazis when he defeated the US boxer, Joe Louis, in 1936. He hid two Jewish friends in his flat for several months.

SOURCE 20 A boy sitting reading on a park bench in Germany, around 1935. The sign painted on it reads 'Only for Aryans'.

SOURCE 18 Franz Six, quite a high ranking SS officer, was put into one of the *Einsatzgruppen* (SS squads which carried out mass killings of Jews in Poland and Russia; see page 40). He later said:

During the war a person could at least try to have himself transferred from an Einsatzgruppe. I myself managed to do this successfully . . . I was not demoted as a result of my transfer and not disadvantaged, apart from remaining on very bad terms with Heydrich [see page 45] until his death.

6

SHOULD BRITAIN HAVE DONE MORE TO HELP GERMAN JEWS?

Evaluate British immigration policy in the 1930s

Ever since the Holocaust people have asked questions about how it could have been avoided. Some people say that more Jews should have been allowed into friendly countries such as Britain. Others say that this criticism is not justified. See what you think.

◆ British immigration policy, 1933–38

In the first five years of Nazi rule, almost half a million Jews left Germany. Twenty per cent went to the USA, ten per cent to Britain.

Britain had 'golden rules' about refugees. British law said that foreigners would be allowed into Britain only if:

◆ they were on their way to somewhere else
◆ they had something to offer Britain, as skilled professionals or business people
◆ they were willing to work as servants
◆ someone else put up money so that the immigrants would not become a burden.

There was no such thing as 'asylum'. The government did not recognise that people might need to flee a country because they were suffering religious, political or racial persecution.

This policy favoured middle-class German Jews. Up to half of those allowed to settle in Britain were professionals such as doctors, dentists or university lecturers. Some of these went on to make enormous contributions to British life, such as Ernst Chain, who helped to develop penicillin. Of the rest, thirty per cent were servants, nearly all women. Jewish organisations in Britain (for example, Rothschilds Bank) put up large amounts of money to SPONSOR German Jewish refugees.

◆ British immigration policy after 1938

In March 1938 Hitler took over Austria, which had a large Jewish population. Britain introduced a system of VISAS so that Jews wanting to escape to Britain could apply to passport offices. Each person was assessed against the four criteria listed above. The delays were enormous.

Then, in November 1938, persecution of the Jews in Germany dramatically increased with *Kristallnacht* (see pages 26–27). There was an outcry from concerned people everywhere. In Britain voluntary groups persuaded the British government to allow in, as special refugees, 10,000 Jewish children aged under 17 (but not their parents). They travelled as the *Kindertransport*.

SOURCE 1 Gerta Ambrozek recalls the *Kindertransport*:

The train left Vienna in the early evening. My father placed my small suitcase on the overhead rack and had to leave the train. We children crowded round the window to receive last-minute instructions. Despite the quietly shed tears, the desperate hopelessness of the people left behind was not really grasped by us. The youngest of the children was three years old and the oldest fourteen. Many children were bewildered as they did not understand why they were leaving their homes and their parents, while to others it appeared as though this was some kind of outing. It wasn't clear to us why our parents, standing in small groups on the platform, were quietly sobbing.

British attitudes in the 1930s

Many British people knew what was going on in Germany.

◆ Some were sympathetic to the plight of German Jews and pressurised the British government to change its policy.
◆ Some were openly racist and anti-Semitic, such as Oswald Mosley, leader of the British Union of FASCISTS.
◆ Some wanted to keep strict controls to prevent large numbers of refugees from entering Britain. They were worried about immigrants taking British jobs when there was already a lot of unemployment – see Source 2.
◆ Some were mildly critical of the Nazis, but hardly sympathetic to German Jews – see Source 3.

SOURCE 2 From the *Daily Mail*, 1935.

Once it is known that Britain offered sanctuary to all who cared to come, the floodgates would be open and we would be inundated by thousands seeking a home.

SOURCE 3 The British Prime Minister, Neville Chamberlain, in a letter to his sister Hilda in July 1939, wrote about Nazi treatment of the Jews since *Kristallnacht*:

No doubt Jews aren't a lovable people. I don't care about them myself. But that is not sufficient to explain the POGROM.

◆ *Hindsight*

Now that we know what happened in the Holocaust, it is natural to look back and feel appalled that Britain did not take more refugees. It is natural to ask, for example: why did Britain accept only the children in the *Kindertransport*? Why did it not take in the parents too? These are moral questions and are very important if we are to learn lessons from history.

However, the historian has another important task – to try to see events as viewed by the people at the time. That means trying to judge this period without hindsight. The historian must judge the past according to what people knew at the time rather than what we know now. In 1938:

◆ It *was* known that the Nazis were persecuting Jews in Germany and Austria.
◆ It was *not* known that two years later Hitler would conquer the Netherlands, Belgium and France, endangering the lives of the German Jews who had taken refuge there in the 1930s.
◆ It was *not* known that three years later Hitler would set out to kill all the Jews in Europe.

DISCUSS

1 Martin Gilbert, an expert historian on the Holocaust, has described Britain's policy then as:
'A neutral stance, not a hostile one, but this neutral stance was to cost a multitude of lives.'
Do you think Martin Gilbert is using hindsight?
2 Based on the evidence here, do you think that Britain:
   a) could have done more to help German Jews
   b) should have done more to help German Jews?

ACTIVITY

The issue of refugees is controversial in Britain today, where people from around the world are seeking refuge because they are:

◆ **either** victims of cruel regimes and are persecuted in their home country
◆ **or** victims of poverty in their home country who want a better opportunity for themselves and their children.

Write three 'golden rules' for British policy towards refugees today. Use what you have found out about the 1930s and what you know about the present day.

WHAT DID THE NAZIS DO TO THE JEWS OF EUROPE DURING THE SECOND WORLD WAR?

Examine the evidence on the Holocaust and decide who was responsible for it

It will be clear to you from what you have studied so far that Hitler was violently anti-Jewish. It will also be clear to you that he and other leading Nazis did their best to encourage anti-Jewish hatred among the German people. Bit by bit, they deprived Jews of their rights. They made Jews into non-citizens. They encouraged Nazi supporters to humiliate, to attack and, in some cases, to kill Jews quite openly.

That is the story so far – a terrible and disturbing story. But now, on pages 38–51, you are going to study more evidence about what happened after the outbreak of war in 1939. The persecution of Jews turned into mass murder and GENOCIDE as millions more Jews in Europe came under Nazi control.

One of the first to suffer was Regina Scherer's father.

◆ The testimony of Regina Scherer: part 3

SOURCE 1

At 4.45a.m. on 1 September 1939, the German army invaded Poland. Although we didn't know it at the time, my father had only 89 days left to live. On 28 November, the twenty Jewish men who were on the Hrubieszow city council (my home town) were called to a special meeting. My mother begged him not to go. Father probably thought that if he didn't go there would be trouble for his family. So he went. All the councillors went. They were ushered into the building through the front entrance and then they were put in a wagon at the back entrance.

We heard what happened from some young boys. The men were led to a clearing in the woods. The boys followed them at a distance and then climbed some trees to witness what happened. Each man was given a spade and told to start digging. When the pit was deep enough they handed the spades back to the soldiers. Then they were told to walk with their hands behind their heads to the edge of the pit they had just dug. My father must have known what was to happen because one boy told my mother that he begged for his life and told the soldiers that he had four children. Of course the soldiers took no notice. Each man was shot in the back of the head. If they didn't fall into the pit they were pushed. If they didn't die immediately, they were suffocated when the soldiers shovelled the freshly dug earth over their bodies.

Much worse was to follow. Over the next six years the Nazis used a range of methods to kill Jews and the other people whom they regarded as enemies of the German state.

NAZI METHODS

1 About 3000 soldiers, in units called *Einsatzgruppen*, were sent to shoot Jews living in Poland and western Russia.

2 Jews from all over eastern Europe were forced into **ghettos** in cities, where they had to live in unhealthy, overcrowded conditions with very little food.

3 Jews were sent by train from all over Europe to concentration camps, where they were worked to death as **slave labour** or killed in specially built **gas chambers**.

◆ *Preparing for your final task*

Throughout this book you have been compiling a source bank of evidence about the Nazi persecution of Jewish people. You have investigated eye-witness accounts, official documents, photographs, memoirs and biographies as well as the work of historians. You have considered this evidence very carefully and used some important historical skills in the process. Much of the evidence and the skills will come in very useful for your final task on page 52, but you need to prepare for it now.

ACTIVITY

This is your challenge.

In a recent court case a judge, Mr Justice Gray, was not judging whether a criminal was guilty; he was judging whether a historian had told the truth. This historian had said that:

1 There was no firm evidence that the Nazis **planned** to kill the Jewish population of Europe.
2 There was no firm evidence that **Hitler** ordered the slaughter of 6 million Jews.
3 There was no firm evidence that Jews were killed in **gas chambers** at Auschwitz camp.

Mr Gray was asked to decide whether the historian was 'bending the evidence' to suit his point of view. He needed to find, and then evaluate, the evidence.

You are going to join Mr Gray's quest for the truth about the Holocaust. As you work through pages 38–51, make notes and gather evidence under these three headings.

EVIDENCE THAT . . .		
. . . the slaughter was planned by the Nazis	. . . Hitler was personally responsible	. . . gas chambers were used to kill Jews at Auschwitz

To get you started, what evidence is there in Source 1 for column 1?

Keep adding to your table as you work, then at the end of this enquiry you will return to the task to write a report for Mr Justice Gray.

◆ *Method 1:* the SS Einsatzgruppen

In 1939, in peacetime, there were 350,000 Jews in Nazi Germany. As the Nazis invaded first Poland and then Russia, millions more Jews came under their control. By the end of 1941 there were around 6 million Jews living in German-occupied territory.

As the German army moved through eastern Europe, it was followed by the SS *Einsatzgruppen* – special squads of soldiers whose job was to round up and shoot Jews and other 'undesirables'. Regina Scherer's father was one of the first people to be murdered like this (see Source 1 on page 38). Often the SS *Einsatzgruppen* would be helped by local anti-Semitic groups who would tell them where to find Jews.

SOURCE 2 After the invasion of Russia in 1941 – quoted in Michael Berenbaum (ed.) *Witness to the Holocaust*, 1997.

Some 3000 men in all [members of the SS Einsatzgruppen] were dispatched on special assignments. Their task was to kill the Jews on the spot – but not only Jews; Communists, Gypsies, political leaders and the INTELLIGENTSIA *were also killed.*

The army invasion was followed up immediately by the round-up of Jews and other intended victims. Those rounded up were marched to the outskirts of the city where they were shot. Their bodies were buried in mass graves – large ditches were filled with bodies of people who had been shot one by one and buried layer upon layer.

Before this phase of the killing ended, more than 1.2 million Jews were killed.

SOURCE 3 Nazis heading for Poland. The words painted on the side of the train read 'We are off to Poland to thrash the Jews'.

Website task

Study Sources 2–6 carefully.

1 List four facts that everyone should know about the work of the SS *Einsatzgruppen*.

2 Select two sources that, in your opinion, provide the most valuable evidence to prove that the work of the SS *Einsatzgruppen* was part of a plan to destroy the Jews of Europe. Explain why you have chosen these sources.

3 Put your descriptions and chosen sources in your website file. Fill out a source data record for each one.

SOURCE 4 Photograph of an execution of Romanian Jews, carried out on 14 September 1941 by members of an SS *Einsatzgruppe*.

SOURCE 5 Testimony of a metalworker from Bremerhaven, a member of Reserve Police Battalion 101, one of the *Einsatzgruppen*.

It was possible for me to shoot only children. It so happened that the mother led the children by the hand. My neighbour then shot the mother and I shot the child that belonged to her because I reasoned with myself that, after all, without its mother the child could not live any longer. It was supposed to be, so to speak, soothing to my conscience to release children unable to live without their mothers.

SOURCE 6 Testimony of SS Obersturmführer (first lieutenant) August Hafner.

I went to the woods alone. The army had already dug a grave. The children were brought along in a tractor. The children were taken down from the tractor. They were lined up along the top of the grave and shot so that they fell into it. The wailing was indescribable. I shall never forget the scene throughout my life. I find it very hard to bear.

I particularly remember a small fair-haired girl who took me by the hand. She too was shot later . . . The grave was near some woods. Many children were hit four or five times before they died.

◆ *Method 2: the ghettos*

Over a million Jews were forced into ghettos in Poland, Czechoslovakia, Hungary and Lithuania. In Warsaw over 500,000 Jews were packed into a tiny area of streets and houses. Every room had to have ten occupants. When the ghetto was full, the Nazis built a high brick wall to shut them all in.

It was only Jews who were forced into ghettos. The rest of the non-Jewish population was allowed to carry on as normal – or as normal as life can be under war conditions.

Conditions inside the ghettos were dreadful. There was no heat, light or running water. Food was almost impossible to buy. Hundreds of thousands of people died of disease and malnutrition. If people tried to leave the ghettos, they were shot by the German guards.

Despite these appalling conditions the Jews still managed to retain some humanity. For example, in August 1942 education was declared illegal in the ghettos. So secret schools were organised and young children crept out of their homes at night to attend them.

SOURCE 7 Photograph of young children in the Warsaw ghetto, 1941.

SOURCE 8 Photograph of a secret school in the Warsaw ghetto.

Jewish resistance in the Warsaw ghetto

From early 1942 thousands of people were taken from the Warsaw ghetto each week. They were sent by train – deported – to concentration camps, from which they never returned. No one in the ghetto could be sure what happened to their friends. However, they all heard dreadful stories. Some, who had contact with the outside world, guessed that they had been taken away to be killed.

In the autumn of 1942 only 40,000 Jews, out of the original 500,000, were still alive in the Warsaw ghetto. For a short time the deportations ceased. Then, when they heard that these were starting again in the spring of 1943, people in the ghetto decided to die fighting instead of accepting deportation. They had managed to keep in touch with members of the RESISTANCE outside of the ghetto and had built up a tiny store of weapons. They had 90 pistols and 500 hand grenades.

On 19 April 1943, the first night of Passover, Nazi soldiers arrived in the ghetto to deport a number of Jews. They were greeted with pistol shots and hand grenades.

Website task

Study Sources 7–10 carefully.

Source 9 has been included as the authors feel that it contains important evidence, but as you can see, the exact origin of the Source has not been established.

1 Who do you think might have written Source 9? What LOADED LANGUAGE leads you to this conclusion?

2 List four facts that everyone should know about the ghettos.

3 Select two sources that, in your opinion, provide the most valuable evidence to prove that the use of ghettos was part of a plan to destroy the Jews of Europe. Explain why you have chosen these sources.

4 Put your descriptions and chosen sources in your website file. Fill out a source data record for each one.

SOURCE 9

Practically unarmed, the population, consisting for the most part of women and children, held off all the might that the Germans could muster – their tanks, their field guns and their airplanes. Most of the ghetto was soon set on fire . . . On the forty-second day of fighting, only one house remained still standing, and the few surviving Jews contested [fought for] every floor until none was left to fight. Warsaw, the Nazis triumphantly announced, was at last 'free of Jews'.

ACTIVITY

Write a description of, or a poem about, the experiences of Jewish people in the Warsaw ghetto.

SOURCE 10 Photograph of Jewish resistance fighters being shot in Chelm, Poland, May 1942.

◆ *Method 3: concentration camps*

Concentration camps had been used by the Nazis since 1933. To start with, they sent their political opponents, such as Communists, there and tortured them. But from 1939 new camps were built. One was at Auschwitz in Poland.

These camps held not only Jews but also Gypsies, political prisoners, disabled people, homosexuals and any other group that was thought to be a threat to the Nazi regime.

At first the method used to kill people in the concentrations camps was quite simple. They were worked to death. They were given very little food – starvation rations – and forced to do back-breaking labour. Most died of malnutrition, filth and neglect.

SOURCE 11 Photograph of two elderly Gypsies waiting for orders at Belzec concentration camp in Poland, in July 1940. Around 600,000 Jews and thousands of Gypsies were killed at Belzec. Only 19 prisoners came out alive.

SOURCE 12 Photograph of five adults with special needs in their concentration camp uniform at Buchenwald, Germany. After 1942, all such people were taken from their homes or hospitals, sent to the camps and killed there.

◆ The 'Final Solution'

On 3 July 1941, Herman Goering, Marshal of the Reich, head of the GESTAPO and one of Hitler's closest advisers, gave a written order for leading Nazis to develop what he called the 'Final Solution' to the Jewish 'problem'.

This led to the Wannsee Conference at which, in January 1942, a group of Nazi leaders agreed on the 'Final Solution'. They decided to set about killing Jews in special death camps or by adding gas chambers to existing concentration camps. Heinrich Himmler was put in charge of implementing this 'Final Solution'. He was assisted by Reinhard Heydrich.

Heydrich had already organised the ghettos and the *Einsatzgruppen*. He planned the sites of the camps, the methods of killing in gas chambers built to hold 2000 people at once, and the transport, by rail, of Jews from all over Europe.

DISCUSS

Why do you think that most of the special death camps were built outside Germany?

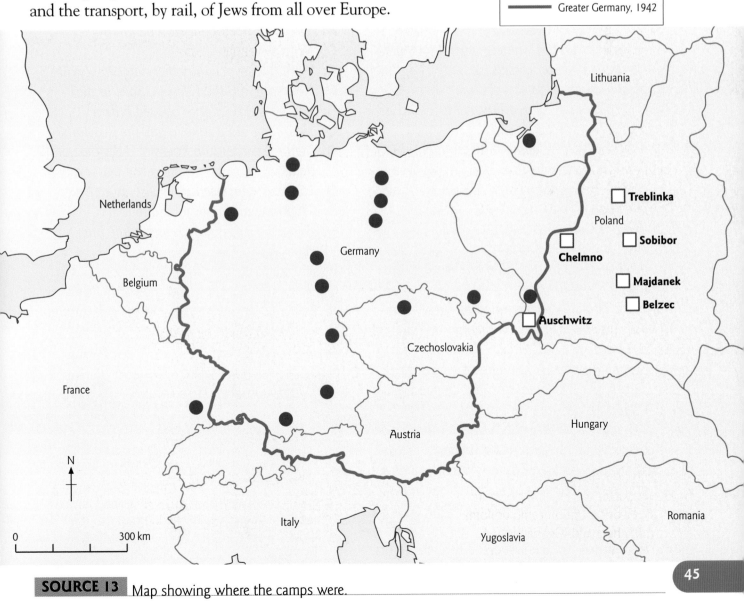

Key
☐ Special death camps
● Concentration camps
— Greater Germany, 1942

SOURCE 13 Map showing where the camps were.

◆ *Implementing 'the Final Solution'*

From the beginning of 1942 onwards, the Nazis used special vans. They called them 'de-lousing vans' and told the Jews they were going to be cleaned so that they entered the vans unsuspectingly. Once they were inside, the doors were locked and gas was let in through holes in the roof.

Soon afterwards large gas chambers were built at a number of concentration camps. In Source 15 a witness describes how the gas was used.

SOURCE 14 Letter to SS Lieutenant-Colonel Rauff, 5 June 1942, Wilhelm Just Section IID 3A Automotive Organisation, Security Police.

Since December 1941, ninety-seven thousand [Jews] have been processed [gassed] using three vans, without any defects showing up in the vehicles. The following adjustments would be useful:

1 In order to ease the rapid distribution of CO [carbon monoxide], two slots, ten by one centimetres, will be bored at the top of the rear wall.

2 The pipe that connects the exhaust to the van tends to rust because it is eaten away from the inside by liquids that flow into it. To avoid this, the nozzle should ... point downward.

3 To facilitate the cleaning of the vehicle, an opening will be made in the floor to allow for drainage.

4 Experience shows that when the back door is closed and it gets dark inside, the load [Jews inside the van] pushes hard against the door. The reason for this is that, when it becomes dark inside, the load rushes towards what little light remains. This hampers the locking of the door. It has also been noticed that the noise provoked by the locking of the door is linked to the fear aroused by the darkness. It is therefore expedient [better] to keep the lights on before the operation and during the first few minutes of its duration.

SOURCE 15 From the testimony of SS Unterscharführer (corporal) Wilhelm Bahr at his trial at Hamburg.

Q: *Is it correct that you have gassed 200 Russian POWs [prisoners of war] with Zyklon B?*

A: *Yes, on orders.*

Q: *On whose order?*

A: *The local doctor, Dr Von Bergmann.*

Q: *With what gas?*

A: *With Prussic acid [another name for Zyklon B].*

Q: *How long did the Russians take to die?*

A: *I do not know. I only obeyed orders.*

Q: *How long did it take to gas the Russians?*

A: *I returned after two hours and they were all dead.*

Q: *For what purpose did you go away?*

A: *That was during lunch hour.*

Q: *You left for your lunch and came back afterwards?*

A: *Yes.*

Q: *Why did you apply the gas to the Russians?*

A: *I only had orders to pour in the gas and I do not know anything about it.*

Website task

Study Sources 14 and 15 carefully.

1 List four facts that everyone should know about the 'Final Solution'.

2 Select one source that, in your opinion, provides the most valuable evidence to prove that the 'Final Solution' was part of a plan to destroy the Jews of Europe. Explain why you have chosen this source.

3 Put your description and chosen source in your website file and fill out a source data record.

◆ *The testimony of Regina Scherer: part 4*

Just one of the millions of people caught up in the 'Final Solution' was Regina Scherer. She spent two and a half years in concentration camps from the age of sixteen to eighteen.

◆ First, she was at Auschwitz.
◆ In January 1945 she was on the Death March that ended up at Mauthausen for two weeks.
◆ From March 1945 she was at Bergen-Belsen until it was liberated by British soldiers in April 1945.

On pages 47–51 is the rest of Regina's story, with illustrations that were drawn by fourteen-year-old Helga Weissova from Czechoslovakia. Helga came from the ghetto of Theresienstadt and spent time at both Auschwitz and Bergen-Belsen. Both Helga and Regina survived to tell their stories.

SOURCE 16

The final solution

Within weeks of my father's death our house had been confiscated and given to Polish Nazis. Our new home had only one room, the floor boards were breaking up, there was one bed, no toilet, no running water, no way of heating and of course no longer any way of growing our own food. With only one bed, the five of us had to sleep head to toe and, with no running water, we could only wash ourselves properly once a month.

One day my mother came home with a piece of pork fat. 'Eat it,' she said. I was horrified and said, 'But, Mummy, this is pork fat. I can't eat it. It is against our religion.' My mother replied, 'Life is more important than anything else.' I have always remembered these words and whenever I was forced to do terrible things in the concentration camps, or whenever I felt like giving up, I would remember my mother's words and they would give me strength to carry on.

One day in June 1942 I came home from work. I was with several other girls. As soon as we arrived back and heard the silence we knew exactly what had happened. We ran to the railway station. It was about three miles away.

Sure enough, our families were there, locked up inside open cattle wagons.

One of the policemen told me that my mother had left me a message, a written message. He said she handed it over to another policeman, that an SS man saw it, took it away, and tore it up. I still don't know to this day what was in the letter, but I believe that my mother wanted to tell me that I should stay alive to bear witness. 'Live to tell the world' is what Mother would have written.

So, my 37-year-old mother, 12-year-old sister, 10-year-old brother and 7-year-old sister were transported to the Belzec extermination camp. After days of living hell, cooped up in a filthy, freezing cattle truck with no food or water, they stepped off the train and, since they would have been either too young or too ill to work, were sent straight to the gas chambers. Each child suffered intolerable indignities. Mother must have been glad to die and glad to know that at least she was with them to the end, comforting and cajoling [encouraging] them as they bade farewell to the cruel world that had rejected them almost from birth.

SOURCE 17

The journey to Auschwitz, February 1943

I remember the date, 2 February 1943, when I heard that I was to be transported to Auschwitz. I joined a convoy of 160 prisoners. We arrived in the town of Auschwitz at 2 o'clock in the morning. It was cold and there was nobody to meet us, so we walked. As we walked through the entrance, under the sign 'Arbeit macht frei [Work makes you free]', there were three men hanging from gallows.

I knew I was in hell.

Their intention was to dehumanise us. They took our clothes and made us stand naked. Each person stepped forward to have a number tattooed on their wrist. Mine was 34679. Then they shaved all our hair off. We huddled together to keep warm and to protect our modesty. A German guard began laughing at us.

'You will soon forget that behaviour,' he laughed. 'Soon you will behave like animals to each other.

Then you will die.' I looked at him and said, 'There is a saying, "Clothes make people," but I personally have never believed that.' He looked hard at me. 'Fighting words for a Jew,' he said. 'But I won't kill you yet. I shall wait two weeks. Then I will come and find you ... if you are still alive.' I knew then that I would live. Never, never would this man have the satisfaction of seeing my corpse.

A guard handed out our camp clothes: a coarse cotton jacket; a pair of trousers; no underwear. Nothing to protect our skin from the lice which, as our bodies warmed up, jumped from the seams of the clothes and burrowed beneath our skin. A large bundle of wooden clogs was thrown into the middle of the floor. Everyone scrambled to find a pair that fitted. Not that it really mattered. These so-called shoes were just a wooden sole with two straps of cloth sewn across for you to slide your feet into.

SOURCE 18 In the barracks (prisoners' building) in Auschwitz.

SOURCE 19

The selection

In the spring of 1943 the infamous [vile] Doctor Mengele joined the camp. He was ready to sort us out again. Mengele took us outside, in the snow, and made us stand there for several hours – no food, no nothing. Then he arrived and stood there with a riding crop [whip] in his hand. He ordered us to line up and to slowly walk in front of him. He looked us up and down and then pointed with his crop. Some went to the right, some went to the left. The line of people sent to the right was much longer than the line sent to the left. All the weaker young people went to the right. All the older people too.

To the right, to the left, to the right, to the left, to death, to life. To the gas chambers, back to the block [barrack]. I was sent to the left . . . back inside the huge gates, and over to the block. Out of 160 people on my particular convoy, only 20 were now left. I thanked God for the person who had told me, 'Scrape your nails on the inside of your hand until it draws blood. Then wipe the blood on your cheeks. It will make you look healthy. The Nazis want healthy, strong people to work for them.'

SOURCE 20 Selection

SOURCE 21

The triumph of good over evil

Being at Auschwitz was like being in hell. I remember so many dreadful things. But I remember equally as clearly so many kind, good and unselfish acts from people I hardly knew who were surviving in just as appalling conditions as myself. I am alive today because of these simple acts of human kindness and because the Nazis failed to destroy the essence of humanity, our human spirit.

Every morning we were woken up to attend roll call. There were several thousand prisoners in the camp at any one time. We all had to go outside and line up one behind the other. We had to stand like this until every single inmate of the camp had been counted. This included all those who had died during the night. Sometimes this would take up to five hours. You can imagine how we felt in the middle of winter. The people in my hut used to help one another. We would stand as close to the person in front as we could and then we would use our warm breath to breathe on to the back of their necks. Everyone would take it in turn to stand at the very back of the line, where there was no one to warm your neck for you. So, you see, we were beating the Nazis yet again. We kept our humanity.

SOURCE 22

Leaving Auschwitz

During the final months of 1944, the SS were preoccupied [busy] with destroying all evidence of Hitler's 'Final Solution'. The gas chambers were destroyed, the ground levelled and trees were planted in their place. Then they began emptying the camp of all remaining prisoners. Each day, fresh convoys of prisoners were sent off in cattle trucks to an unknown destination. When, in January 1945, it was my turn to be moved, the SS had run out of trucks so our convoy was forced to set off on foot. We had no idea where we were going, or how long it would take.

For the entire march, we had only our wooden clogs and our camp uniforms. No coats, no warmer clothing, no boots. Every time the Russian planes flew overhead, we had to hide in ditches by the side of the road. Many people, once they had lain down, were too ill to stand up again. So the SS guards shot them.

SOURCE 23
Death March

SOURCE 24

Survival

It was on this march that I encountered human kindness from the strangest source of all. One evening, the line of 'refugees' was approaching a small village. We were mortally cold and hungry. A female guard, SS Baker, called me out of line to ask about some of the other female prisoners from the kitchens. I couldn't answer her, but by the time she had finished with me, the line had moved on. So she took me to a small cottage at the edge of the village where some of the guards were to spend the night. Her husband was also a guard. He opened the door.

'You have a dirty Jew with you,' her husband hissed. 'Why don't we shoot her?'

'She is in my charge,' SS Baker replied, 'and I will make sure that she remains unharmed.'

That night I slept in a bed alongside three female German SS guards. Yet again my life was saved by an act of kindness. And this person was German, the enemy of all Jews.

On 15 April 1945, the British liberated Belsen, the camp where I finally ended up. I remember the moment the first soldiers walked through the gates of the camp. A prisoner was kneeling just outside these gates. He had a human ear in his mouth, but he was too exhausted even to chew it. The final few days before liberation had seen many prisoners desperately trying to stay alive by eating the flesh of their dead comrades.

The next thing I remember is climbing up one of the watch towers with as big a block of concrete as I could manage to carry. I wanted to drop it on to the head of the camp doctor, Doctor König. But something stopped me. I could not do it. Even after everything I had gone through I knew it was wrong to deliberately harm another human being. I knew that if I did, then the Nazis would have won. They would have dehumanised me after all.

SOURCE 25

After the liberation

People often ask me if I can forgive the Nazis for what happened. This is what I say to them. I can try to forgive what they did to me, but I have no right to forgive, or to forget, what they did to my mother, father, two sisters and brother. Only they can forgive. My mother and father had always taught me that the person who hates is eventually destroyed by his own hatred. I lost all hope in Auschwitz and Bergen-Belsen but I never lost my human spirit. I never lost my sense of what is right and wrong and I never learned to hate as Hitler and the Nazis hated.

ACTIVITY

Study Sources 16–25.

1 On your own copy of Regina's testimony highlight all the important information that you think should be seen by Mr Justice Gray as he tries to understand what took place in the camps.

2 Use the information from Regina's testimony to write captions for Helga's drawings so that it becomes clear what is happening in them.

DISCUSS

How could you use Regina's testimony on your website?

◆ *Your final task*

You are following in the footsteps of a real trial that took place in the year 2000.

Mr Justice Gray had to judge whether a historian had told the truth. This historian had said that:

1 There was no firm evidence that the Nazis **planned** to kill the Jewish population of Europe.
2 There was no firm evidence that **Hitler** ordered the slaughter of 6 million Jews.
3 There was no firm evidence that Jews were killed in **gas chambers** at Auschwitz camp.

Mr Gray was asked to decide whether the historian was 'bending the evidence' to suit his point of view. He needed to find, and then evaluate, the evidence.

ACTIVITY

You are now going to help the judge. You have been collecting ideas over pages 38–51. You have probably got quite a lot of evidence for issues 1 and 3 but probably not much about issue 2. Your final task is to pick either issue 1 or issue 3 and to select five pieces of evidence which you have studied that *in your opinion* provide the most useful and reliable evidence about that issue.

Write a report for Mr Justice Gray. For each piece of evidence explain *why* you have chosen it, and evaluate its reliability.

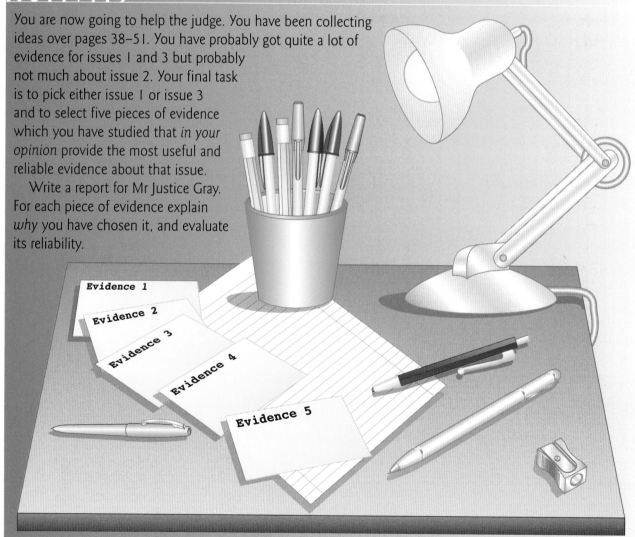

Evidence 1
Evidence 2
Evidence 3
Evidence 4
Evidence 5

Issue 2: was Hitler himself responsible?

This is the hardest point to prove.

It is quite difficult to pin down responsibility for the Holocaust in a way that would stand up in a court of law. Hitler rarely wrote down orders or instructions. His close colleagues gave orders. They were perhaps following instructions from Hitler or perhaps acting on their own but in line with what they thought that Hitler would want. Most of the documents that might have told us were burnt by the Nazis in 1945, in the last days of the war.

However, there is no doubt about the wishes of Hitler.

> **SOURCE 26** Adolf Hitler, 1919.
>
> *Anti-Semitism on purely emotional grounds will find its expression in pogroms. However, rational anti-Semitism's final, unalterable objective must be the removal of the Jews altogether.*

That was in 1919. He said many similar things afterwards. You can find more examples on page 17. He set the agenda that his deputies then followed. His HENCHMEN who carried out the 'Final Solution' **believed that they were carrying out the instructions of the Führer.**

Justice Gray's conclusion

At his summing up Justice Gray said that having looked at all the evidence presented, no objective, fair-minded historian could doubt the Holocaust. There was no doubt in his mind that the historian that had denied these events was anti-Jewish and because of that had tried to bend the evidence and play down the role of Hitler in the Holocaust.

The Nuremberg Trials

Hitler committed suicide in April 1945, just a few days before the end of the war, so he was never put on trial. Of the other key figures involved in the 'Final Solution', Himmler was captured by the British in 1945 but he too killed himself, and Heydrich was assassinated by Czech resistance fighters in 1942. However, Goering and other Nazi leaders were put on trial. At the International War Crimes Tribunal in Nuremberg, 21 Nazis were tried together to find out:

- ◆ Who was responsible for the Holocaust?
- ◆ Who gave the orders?
- ◆ Was there a common conspiracy to commit these terrible crimes against humanity?
- ◆ Can a statesman who leads people into war be held personally responsible?

The judges at the Tribunal eventually decided that:
'The crimes of international law are committed by men. Only by punishing individuals who commit such crimes can international law be enforced.'

So, eleven of the accused were sentenced to be hanged, seven received life imprisonment and three were freed.

> **SOURCE 27** Some of the accused at the Nuremberg International War Crimes Tribunal. Herman Goering, seated at the front on the left, took poison after he was sentenced.

8 WHO RESISTED HITLER?

Many did resist Nazism. What would you have done?

As you were reading this book, you may well have thought: why didn't someone try to stop the Nazis? Of course, many did. But it was not easy: Hitler had complete control over Germany and the lands he conquered across Europe. The Nazis were ruthless towards their opponents, but millions of ordinary people risked or gave their lives to oppose them.

ACTIVITY

As you read about those who did resist in different ways, think about what you would have done in their situation. Be honest.

Young people

When Hitler invaded Poland in September 1939, many young Jews went into hiding. They formed 'PARTISAN groups' to fight against the Germans in any way they could.

TO RESIST WAS . . .

✓ To smuggle a loaf of bread
✓ To teach in secret
✓ To cry out warning and shatter illusions
✓ To rescue a Torah scroll [a very precious religious symbol]
✓ To forge [fake] documents
✓ To smuggle people across borders
✓ To chronicle [write down] events and conceal the records
✓ To hold out a helping hand to the needy
✓ To contact those under siege and smuggle weapons
✓ To fight with weapons in the streets, mountains and forests
✓ To rebel in death camps
✓ To rise up in ghettos, among the crumbling walls, in the most desperate revolt.

SOURCE 1 A list of actions by Jews that were, in some way, to resist the Nazis. The list is displayed in the 'Ghetto Fighters' House' in Acre, Israel, a museum built to tell of the Holocaust.

Many of these actions meant an automatic sentence of death if the young people carrying them out were caught by the Nazis. The executions were usually carried out in public and local people were forced to watch.

SOURCE 2 On 26 July 1941, in Minsk, Belarus, three young Russian Jews, Masha Bruskina (*centre*), Volodya Sherbateivich and Krill Trous, were taken to be publicly hanged by the Nazis. The sign around Masha's neck reads, 'We are partisans [armed resistance]. We shot at the German army.'

Masha Bruskina was a high school graduate aged seventeen. She worked as a nurse in a military hospital. She was a member of a resistance group which aided Russian officers, who were patients there, to escape and join the partisans. The members of the group were informed on, caught and hanged.

Some resistance fighters were recruited by Britain. One such person was seventeen-year-old Hannah Sennesh, a Hungarian Jew who had emigrated to Palestine, where she was living in safety with her family. Despite this, Hannah agreed to be dropped by parachute into Hungary to organise partisan resistance to the Germans. But Hannah was betrayed, tortured and finally executed, in November 1944.

Prisoners

Jews who were forced into the ghettos also found the strength to rebel against the Germans. In 1943, there was a huge revolt in the Warsaw ghetto in Poland (see page 43). Eventually, however, the Germans overcame this resistance and killed everyone who was involved.

Even in the death camps, the Jews found courage to resist the Nazis. One of the best examples of bravery came from the Jews in Auschwitz who were forced to become *Sonderkommando* (the people who emptied the bodies from the gas chambers). One day, as the war was drawing to a close, they managed to blow up two of the gas chambers before they were killed by the Nazi guards. In this way, the *Sonderkommando* knew that they were saving the lives of several thousand Jews in the camp, perhaps long enough for them to be rescued by British or Russian soldiers.

SOURCE 3 Before she died, Hannah Sennesh wrote this poem.

Blessed is the match that is consumed in kindling flame
Blessed is the flame that burns in the secret places of the heart
Blessed is the heart with strength to stop its beating for honour's sake
Blessed is the match that is consumed in kindling flame.

Germans who resisted Hitler

Bonhoeffer and Protestant resistance

Dietrich Bonhoeffer was a Protestant church minister. As a Christian, he was against Nazism from the first. He argued that it was one's religious duty to hold to one's beliefs and not to give way to a political idea. Before the war he visited Britain and the USA to warn of the dangers of Nazism. Although friends there wanted him to stay, he always returned to Germany so that he could join in Protestant resistance to the Nazis. He was arrested in 1943, put in prison and then transferred to a labour camp at Buchenwald in 1944. He was executed in April 1945.

The White Rose Group

In 1943, five young university students – Hans and Sophie Scholl, Christoph Probst, Willi Graf and Alexander Schmorell – along with Professor Kurt Huber, a professor of philosophy at Munich University – formed a group calling themselves the 'White Rose'. The students had all grown up knowing only Hitler as their Führer. They had been indoctrinated by the Hitler Youth and had each spent a year serving in the German army.

SOURCE 5 Hans' sister, Inge Scholl, remembers that as early as 1935 her family realised that the Nazis were dangerous:

Hans had been promoted to the rank of troop leader in the Hitler Youth. He and his troop had designed a special banner dedicated to the Führer, and the boys had pledged their loyalty to the banner because it was the symbol of their fellowship. One evening, however, the group leader suddenly ordered the little flag bearer, a cheerful twelve year old, to hand over the banner:

'You don't need a banner of your own. Use the one ordered for everyone.'

The order was repeated and the boy stood rigid. Hans noticed that the flag was trembling. At that he lost control. He quietly stepped from his place in the ranks and slapped the group leader.

. . . Then we heard a story about a young teacher who had unaccountably disappeared. He had been ordered to stand before a squad [of Stormtroopers] and each man was ordered to pass by the teacher and to spit in his face. After that incident no one saw him again. He had disappeared into a concentration camp. 'What did he do?' we asked his mother in bewilderment. 'Nothing. Nothing,' she cried out in despair. 'He just wasn't a Nazi, it was impossible for him to belong. That was his crime.'

SOURCE 4 Hans Scholl (*left*), his sister Sophie Scholl, and Christoph Probst in Munich, 1942.

By 1943, Hans was 25 years old and studying medicine at university in Munich. Sophie, his younger sister, was studying philosophy. Their aim in forming the 'White Rose', was to destroy Nazism. The group had posters printed outlining their beliefs and scattered them all over the university campus. Early one morning members of the group painted the words 'Down with Hitler' on walls across the city. Over the front doors of the university, they painted the word 'Freedom'. News of this rebellion spread quickly. Brave young students in other universities began to do similar things under the banner of the 'White Rose'. Every one involved knew that they faced certain death.

On 21 February 1943, the six founders of the White Rose Group were arrested by the Gestapo. Even though they knew others had supported them, they took all the blame themselves and admitted everything. The Scholls and Christoph Probst were tried first and were sentenced to death by beheading. A few days later, the other three founders of the group were tried and executed.

SOURCE 6 Hans' sister describes what happened to three of the defendants, Hans and Sophie Scholl and Christoph Probst:

Calm and upright in their seats, and very much alone, the three young defendants sat opposite. They gave their replies openly and deliberately. Sophie said, 'What we said and wrote is what many people are thinking. Only they don't dare to say it.'

They were found guilty and sentenced to death.

My parents had the miraculous good fortune of being able to visit their children once more.

First Hans was brought out. He was in prison uniform, he walked upright and briskly, and he allowed nothing in the circumstances to becloud his spirit. He took his parents' hands.

'I have no hatred. I have put everything, everything behind me.'

My father embraced him and said, 'You will go down in history – there is such a thing as justice in spite of all this.'

Then Sophie was brought in . . . She too was noticeably thinner but her face revealed a marvellous sense of triumph.

'So now you will never again set foot in our house,' said Mother.

'Oh, what do these few short years matter, Mother?' she answered . . . 'We took all the blame for everything. That is bound to have its effect in time to come.'

The prison guards told us what happened next.

'They were led off, the girl first. She went without the flicker of an eyelash. None of us understood how this was possible. The executioner said he had never seen anyone meet their end as she did.'

And Hans – before he placed his head on the block – Hans called out so that the words rang through the huge prison: 'Long live freedom!'

ACTIVITY

The Yad Vashem Holocaust Memorial Museum in Jerusalem has a special garden to remember those non-Jews who helped the Jews during that period. Oskar Schindler, a German businessman who employed Jews to save them from being transported to the death camps (and whose story was told in the film *Schindler's List*), has a memorial plaque in this garden.

Write a letter to the Director of the museum explaining why the six German members of the White Rose Group should also be included in this garden.

SO ... WHY DID IT HAPPEN?

Assess the factors that brought about the Holocaust

Now that you have worked your way through this book, you know that the reasons for the Holocaust spread out far beyond Adolf Hitler. Indeed, although he must be at the centre of any explanation, it is unlikely that he ever personally killed any Jews and it is even quite difficult to pin down the moment when he ordered the Holocaust. The explanation widens in various directions:

PEOPLE

The orders for the Holocaust came from senior Nazis. However, these orders were carried out down the chain of command by ordinary people: guards ran the camps, clerks recorded names, engine drivers drove the trains to the camps, bricklayers built the gas chambers, chemical workers made the poison gas. And by no means all these people were Germans. Camp guards included Poles, Lithuanians, Russians, Ukrainians and others. Police in occupied countries rounded up Jews on German orders without complaint: French, Italian, Russian, Romanian, Greek and others, even British police in the occupied Channel Islands.

HITLER

Hitler was a strong charismatic leader with total power. He was strongly anti-Semitic – he passed laws against Jews and attempted to brainwash the German people against them.

OPPOSITION

Perhaps other countries could have done more to prevent the Holocaust; perhaps the German people should have protested more; perhaps Jews should have resisted more.

HISTORY

Anti-Semitism dates back many centuries. In the nineteenth century it changed from a religious to a non-religious racism, but was still present in many countries.

Why...?

INDUSTRY

Twentieth-century industrial methods gave the Nazis the ability to mechanise death. The railway network and the construction and chemical industries put the Holocaust into effect in a way that would have been impossible in previous centuries.

THE WAR

Although Hitler and the Nazis were attacking Jews in Germany well before the Second World War, it was the war which brought many millions more Jews under Nazi rule. The war also made death and killing more common and forced many people to get used to taking orders.

DISCUSS

1 Look at Source 1. Which people made decisions that led to Anny-Yolande Horowitz becoming a victim of the Holocaust?

2 The photograph on page 58 shows the railway track into Auschwitz. Which people might have been involved in getting the railway built and in getting the trains safely to Auschwitz?

3 a) Are any of the people you have listed in questions 1 and 2 to blame for the Holocaust?

   b) If so, how much are they to blame?

SOURCE 1 Identity card of Anny-Yolande Horowitz, a French Jewish girl. (*Juive* = French word for a female Jew.) A French clerk issued this card in December 1940 and a French policeman decided she should be put 'under surveillance as a foreigner' (*Étranger Surveillé*), even though she was only seven years old at the time and had been born in Strasbourg, France. She was deported to Auschwitz in 1942.

ACTIVITY: THINKING IT OUT

Here are ten reasons why the Holocaust took place.

◆ Some are **N**: **n**ot true or unimportant.
◆ Some are **P**: they made the Holocaust **p**ossible, but didn't make it happen.
◆ Some are **I**: **i**mportant causes.

Use what you have found out in this book to put **N**, **P** or **I** against each one. If someone disagrees with your decision, you have to find evidence in the book to support what you think.

1 Anti-Semitism had been around for centuries and was present in many European countries.
2 Hitler hated Jews.
3 Many leading Nazis were anti-Semitic.
4 The German people were anti-Semitic.
5 The German people had been brainwashed to think of Jews as non-humans.
6 The German people obeyed orders.
7 Germany was a modern, industrialised country.
8 The Second World War made brutality towards other human beings acceptable.
9 Foreign countries didn't do enough to stop it.
10 The Jews didn't fight back strongly enough.

Afterwards you could:

a) Hold a group discussion on which three reasons were most important in causing the Holocaust.

b) Make a group wall display about the reasons for the Holocaust. You could start by writing what you think is the most important cause in the centre of a large sheet of paper. Write in other important reasons (**I**) nearby. Draw lines linking them. Write in less important reasons and factors which made the Holocaust possible (**P**) near the edge of the sheet. Leave out reasons you think are wrong or unimportant (**N**). Again, use the book to support, or challenge, other people's decisions.

c) Complete Activity b) using the cards which your teacher will give you, laid out on a large sheet of paper.

WHY STUDY THE HOLOCAUST?
Evaluate the historical significance of the Holocaust

Many people think the Holocaust is so important that everyone should know about it.

◆ Young people should learn about it at school: it is one of the few historical events actually named in the National Curriculum.
◆ We should never forget it: the British government declared 27 January 2001 the first Holocaust Memorial Day.

You have spent time studying the Holocaust yourself. What is your opinion?

Speaker 1

By learning about the Holocaust and understanding how it became possible, we can prevent history repeating itself.

Speaker 2

Studying the Holocaust won't help prevent future genocide. Even though no one since 1945 could be ignorant of the Holocaust, there have already been several genocides since then: for example in Kampuchea in the 1970s, and in Rwanda in 1994.

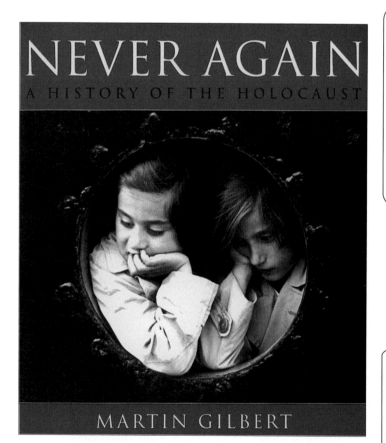

Speaker 3

We study the Holocaust because it is a significant historical event. But it has no special moral lessons for us.

SOURCE 1 Martin Gilbert's book *Never Again*, published in 2000. Why do you think he chose this title?

DISCUSS

1 Which of the speakers, 1–3, do you most agree with?

2 Can you think of any other reasons why we should or should not study the Holocaust?

3 The Chief Rabbi, Jonathan Sacks (a British, Jewish leader) welcomed the Holocaust Memorial Day as a: 'universal reflection on what it is to be human'. What do you think he meant?

ACTIVITY

Very few people doubt that the Holocaust was a significant event. But *why* was it significant? This activity is designed to help you find out.

Each group should take one criterion and use this book and the material on your website to judge whether the Holocaust fulfils the criterion strongly enough to be counted as a really important event in history. The following questions will help you to judge each criterion.

IMPORTANCE
Was it important to people living at the time?

How important was the Holocaust to: Jews in Europe? The Nazis? The German people? People in other countries?

PROFUNDITY
How deeply were people's lives affected?

How did the Holocaust affect the day-to-day lives of the Jews? The Germans? People in other countries? How were people affected individually and as a community? How did it affect future generations?

QUANTITY
How many people were affected?

How many people were taken to concentration camps? How many people were killed during the Holocaust? How many Germans supported the Nazis, and how many resisted? How many were punished for their part in the Holocaust?

DURATION
For how long were people's lives affected?

When did the Holocaust really begin? When did it end? Are some people's lives still affected by the Holocaust today?

RELEVANCE
Is it still relevant to our lives today?

What can we learn from the Holocaust that could help us understand or solve the problems we face in the world today? Have there been any similar events in the world since the Holocaust? Why do you think we have a Holocaust Memorial Day?

CONSEQUENCES
What significant changes did it lead to?

There is not much to help you with this in this book, but here are two unexpected, but important, results of the Holocaust that you could think about.

Jews were helpless victims of the Holocaust. The Holocaust helped lead to the creation of the state of Israel. This was a significant event for the Middle East and for the world.

The Holocaust put an end to the idea that white Europeans had a superior civilisation. When we demanded independence after the war and the Holocaust, many of our colonial rulers soon gave in.

◆ Glossary

ALLOTMENT a small patch of land used by one person, or family, for growing food in cities and places where gardens are small or non-existent

ANTI-SEMITISM hostility towards Jews

ARTEFACT something made by human hands, such as a tool or work of art

ARYAN in Nazi racist thinking, an Aryan was a member of the white, non-Jewish, race

ASSETS valuable possessions, such as goods, property, shares etc.

BOYCOTT to refuse to trade or do business with

COLONIES overseas possessions of another, more developed country, which settles its people there and uses its resources

CONCENTRATION CAMP special prison camp set up by the Nazis to hold their enemies, including Jews

DEPRESSION a decline in the economy of a country, leading to unemployment and falling standards of living

DICTATOR someone who has total personal power over a country

ETHNIC belonging to a particular racial, national or cultural group

EXTREMIST someone who holds intolerant and intense views

FASCISTS extremist nationalist, and often racist, groups, common in 1930s politics

FÜHRER the German word for leader, which Adolf Hitler used as his title

GENOCIDE the systematic killing of people who belong to a particular racial group

GESTAPO state secret police in Nazi Germany. The name is an abbreviation of <u>Ge</u>heime <u>Sta</u>atspolizei

HENCHMEN faithful supporters and friends

INDOCTRINATING teaching a point of view so forcefully that people accept it unthinkingly

INTELLIGENTSIA The most educated people in a country, or society

JUDAISM the religion of the Jewish people

LOADED LANGUAGE words used to give a particular point of view

NAZI a member of the German political party led by Adolf Hitler. The word is an abbreviation of the full name of the party, <u>Nationalso</u>zialistische Deutsche Arbeiterpartei (National Socialist German Workers' Party)

PARTISAN a member of an armed resistance group in a country occupied by an enemy (for example, German-occupied eastern Europe)

PERSECUTED treated badly

POGROM organised attacks on Jews, from Jewish/Russian words meaning 'like thunder'

PREJUDICE a hostile point of view that is not based on fact

PROPAGANDA false or misleading information given out to spread a certain point of view

PUTSCH a German word for an attempt to seize control of the government by force

REPARATIONS compensation paid by a defeated nation for the damage caused during a war. At the end of the First World War the Treaty of Versailles was agreed, which held Germany solely to blame for the war. Initially the compensation was set at £6.6 million, payable mainly to France and Britain

RESISTANCE the name given to people who fought secretly against German occupation of their country (usually in western Europe)

SORCERY black magic, witchcraft

SPONSOR pay for

SS abbreviation for the Schutzstaffel, formed as Hitler's personal bodyguard in 1926, who swore an oath of personal loyalty to him. They wore black and later increased in size until they formed whole army units and ran the concentration camps

STERILISE to operate on a man or woman in order to make them incapable of producing children

TESTIMONY this word is used in law courts, so it means a truthful account, as if given on oath

VISA a special document allowing someone to leave and enter a country

Index

◆ Titles in the series

Pupils' Books (PB) and Teachers' Resource Books (TRB) are available for all titles.

Write Your Own Roman Story	**PB** 0 7195 7717 9	**TRB** 0 7195 7718 7
The Norman Conquest	**PB** 0 7195 8555 4	**TRB** 0 7195 8556 2
King John	**PB** 0 7195 8539 2	**TRB** 0 7195 8540 6
Lost in Time	**PB** 0 7195 8557 0	**TRB** 0 7195 8558 9
'King' Cromwell?	**PB** 0 7195 8559 7	**TRB** 0 7195 8560 0
The Impact of Empire	**PB** 0 7195 8561 9	**TRB** 0 7195 8562 7
Dying for the Vote	**PB** 0 7195 8563 5	**TRB** 0 7195 8564 3
The Trenches	**PB** 0 7195 8565 1	**TRB** 0 7195 8566 X
The Holocaust	**PB** 0 7195 7709 8	**TRB** 0 7195 7710 1
The Twentieth Century	**PB** 0 7195 7711 X	**TRB** 0 7195 7712 8

◆ Acknowledgements

Photographs reproduced by kind permission of:
Cover Yad Vashem Film and Photo Archive; **p.4** *tl & bl* John Townson/Creation, *r* AKG London; **p.5** *t* AKG London, *b* Musée de la Ville de Paris, Musée Carnavalet, Paris, France/Bridgeman Art Library; **p.6** Photo courtesy *Coventry Evening Telegraph*; **p.7** ullstein bild Berlin – Ritter; **p.9** *tl* Photo courtesy Jack Kagan, *tr* ullstein bild Berlin – Minehan, *b* AKG London; **p.10** Photo courtesy *Coventry Evening Telegraph*; **p.13** *tl* © Gianni Dagli Orti/Corbis, *tr & br* AKG London, *bl* AKG London/Erich Lessing; **p.15** Bildarchiv Preussischer Kulturbesitz; **p.16** *t & b* AKG London; **p.17** Bildarchiv Preussischer Kulturbesitz; **p.19** *l* Imperial War Museum, London, *r* Süddeutscher Verlag Bilderdienst; **p.21** *tl* © Bettmann/Corbis, *tr* AKG London, *bl* Imperial War Museum, London (MH13348), *br* William Blye, courtesy of USHMM Photo Archives; **p.23** Hulton Archive; **p.24** Stadtarchiv Bielefeld; **p.27** *t* Trudy Isenberg, courtesy of USHMM Photo Archives, *b* National Archives, courtesy of USHMM Photo Archives; **p.28** AKG London; **p.29** *tl & b* AKG London, *tr* Bundesarchiv Koblenz; **p.31** *tl* Lawrence E. Gichner, courtesy of USHMM Photo Archives, *tr* Courtesy of USHMM Photo Archives, *b* Wiener Library; **p.32** © Hulton-Deutsch Collection/Corbis; **p.33** *t & br* AKG London, *bl* Bildarchiv Preussischer Kulturbesitz; **p.35** *t* AKG London, *b* Hulton Archive; **p.38** Photo courtesy *Coventry Evening Telegraph*; **p.41** Imperial War Museum, London (HU86369); **p.40** Yad Vashem Film and Photo Archive; **p.42** *l* AKG London, *r* Lithuanian Central State Archive; **p.43** Yad Vashem Film and Photo Archive; **p.44** *t* Jerzy Ficowski, courtesy of USHMM Photo Archives, *b* Robert A. Schmuhl, courtesy of USHMM Photo Archives; **p.47** Photo courtesy *Coventry Evening Telegraph*; **pp.48, 49 & 50** From: Helga Weissová, *Zeichne, was Du siehst: Zeichnungen eines Kindes aus Theresienstadt/Terezín/Maluj, co vidíš/Draw What You See*, ed. by Niedersächsische Verein zur Förderung von Theresienstadt/Terezín e. V. © Wallstein Verlag Göttingen, 1998; **p.53** AKG London; **p.55** Bundesarchiv, Koblenz (photo: Ghetto Fighters' House, Israel); **p.56** Bildarchiv Preussischer Kulturbesitz (photo: George J. Wittenstein); **p.58** AKG London/ Michael Teller; **p.60** courtesy HarperCollins.

(*t* = top, *b* = bottom, *l* = left, *r* = right)

Text extracts reproduced by kind permission of:
p.13 *both Anti-Semitism – A History Portrayed*, Anne Frank House; **p.17** Extract from *Mein Kampf* published by Pimlico. Used by permission of The Random House Group Limited; **p.26** © Yad Vashem; **p.30** © Peter Becker, University of South Carolina; **p.32** Courtesy of the German Propaganda Archive (http://www.calvin.edu/academic/cas/gpa/); **p.34** *Source 15* Christopher R. Browning, *The Path to Genocide, Essays on Launching the Final Solution*, 1992, Cambridge University Press, *Source 16* HarperCollins Publishers Ltd © 2000, Martin Gilbert; **p.40** © 1997 by Michael Berenbaum. Reprinted by permission of HarperCollins Publishers Inc; **p.41** © 2001 Christopher R. Browning. Reprinted by permission of HarperCollins Publishers Inc, © Konecky and Konecky; **p.46** © The Beate Klarsfeld Foundation; **p.54** © Ghetto Fighters' House; **p.56–7** © Wesleyan University Press.

While every effort has been made to contact copyright holders, the Publishers apologise for any omissions, which they will be pleased to rectify at the earliest opportunity.